201 Relationship Questions:

The Couple's Guide to Building Trust and Emotional Intimacy

Barrie Davenport

Disclaimer

No part of this publication may be reproduced or transmitted in any form or by any means, mechanical or electronic, including photocopying or recording, or by any information storage and retrieval system, or transmitted by email without permission in writing from the publisher.

While all attempts have been made to verify the information provided in this publication, neither the author nor the publisher assumes any responsibility for errors, omissions, or contrary interpretations of the subject matter herein.

This book is for entertainment purposes only. The views expressed are those of the author alone, and should not be taken as expert instruction or commands. The reader is responsible for his or her own actions.

Adherence to all applicable laws and regulations, including international, federal, state, and local governing professional licensing, business practices, advertising, and all other aspects of doing business in the United States, Canada, or any other jurisdiction is the sole responsibility of the purchaser or reader.

Neither the author nor the publisher assumes any responsibility or liability whatsoever on the behalf of the purchaser or reader of these materials.

Any perceived slight of any individual or organization is purely unintentional.

Your Free Gift

As a way of saying thank you for your purchase, you're invited to enroll in our Relationship Questions Companion Course. I hope you enjoy this free resource.

You can join this free course by going to this site: https://liveboldandbloom.com/free-relationship-course.

Contents

Section 9: Disagreements and Differences... 91

140

About Barrie Davenport

Barrie Davenport is a certified personal coach,
thought leader, author, and creator of several online
courses on self-confidence, life passion, and habit
creation. She is the founder of two top-ranked personal development sites, Live Bold and Bloom.com
and BarrieDavenport.com. Her work as a coach,
blogger, and author is focused on offering people
practical strategies for living happier, more successful, and more mindful lives. She utilizes time-
tested, evidence-based, action-oriented principles
and methods to create real and measurable results
for self-improvement.

You can learn more about Barrie on her Amazon
author page at barriedavenport.com/author.

Introduction

The beginning of love is to let those we love be perfectly themselves, and not to twist them to fit our own image. Otherwise we love only the reflection of ourselves we find in them.

~Thomas Merton

Consider this for a moment: why did you get involved in your love relationship in the first place? Was it, as Merton suggests, to find a reflection of yourself? Were you hoping to find the one person who would complete you and meet your needs? Maybe you were looking for someone to finally make you happy. What were your expectations from love and this person who stands by your side?

Primarily we develop our love relationship because, well, we fall in love. We are magically drawn to this wonderful person who can do no wrong and whose mere presence makes us melt into a puddle of aching desire. We don't tend to think about the "why" of it. When we find love, we're too deliriously happy to consider the reason for our good fortune. Yet behind the powerful, chemically driven feelings of love and attraction are the more practical desires for companionship, emotional intimacy, and a sense of belonging and security.

Not too long ago, we expected a romantic partnership to inevitably lead to marriage, a contract that ensured some financial stability, respectability, and hopefully progeny. Love and sexual chemistry were optional. Today, most people view marriage as a bond between equals grounded in mutual love and respect. Rather than reflecting the unique, gender-based roles of unions just 50 years ago, most marriages today are based on flexible divisions of labor, companionship, and sexual attraction. These evolving views about marriage have paved the way for gay marriage, acceptable cohabitation, and a variety of lifestyle choices for all love relationships.

In fact, marriage itself is becoming increasingly optional, with more people choosing to delay it or avoid it altogether in favor of living together. According to the Pew Research Center, the median age for marriage in the early 1980s was 25 for men and 22 for women. However in 2011, the median ages for first marriages hit a record high of 29 for men and 27 for women. The Pew report found that couples no longer feel the need to be married to become parents and the options of other lifestyles, such as living alone or living with partners, has contributed to delaying marriage. Most divorced people are choosing to avoid marrying again. Only 29 percent of people who have been married before say they'd be willing to take another trip to the altar.

So what do these statistics and the changing views about love and marriage have to do with your committed relationship? The important take-away here is that love relationships are no longer defined by convenience and traditional roles. Whether you are married, living with someone, or dating, you have the freedom to create a deeply satisfying bond based on love, sexual attraction, friendship, intimacy, and mutual respect. Being in a committed, intimate relationship *does* lead to a more satisfying life. According to a Cornell University study, people who are in a committed relationship live longer, are happier in general, and tend to accumulate more wealth. The strongest commitments create the most satisfaction.

But if that's the case, why are relationships often so difficult and painful? Why do we argue, belittle, and disengage from the one person we're supposed to love most? We have more freedom than ever to enjoy a healthy, loving relationship, yet we can't seem to manage conflict and stress with our beloved. The very same person whose gaze left you reeling with passion in the beginning is now the one pushing all your buttons and making you crazy.

I find it ironic that we go through extensive training to drive a car and spend years in school preparing for a career, but there's no expected or required training when it comes to this most vital part of our lives—our love relationship. No one teaches us how to be a good partner, how to nurture the health of the relationship, and how to resolve differences in a mature way. We jump in like blind fools, certain that love will conquer all.

If we're lucky, we had good role models in our parents, but even so, our particular relationship has its own nuances, issues, and unsightly bumps. Once the initial infatuation wears off, we are left with few skills to navigate those bumps and maintain the vitality and joy of the connection. Over time, many couples wind up in their separate corners, scowling at each other from a distance. This certainly isn't what we thought would happen when we first stared at our lover across the room and our hearts melted.

All problems in relationships boil down to one thing: a lack of empathic communication.

Whether our concerns relate to money, sex, kids, affection, career, or any of the various reasons we fight or get angry, when we don't communicate our needs and discuss our differences in the spirit of love, things inevitably break down. You've been there. So have I. We are turf-oriented creatures, even with our most intimate partners. We want to protect what's ours—emotionally, psychologically, and physically—often at the expense of those we love most. Intimate, healthy relationships require letting go of some of that turf and recognizing that the other person's needs and feelings are as valid as our own.

Simply living in the same space with another person provides plenty of fodder for frustration and conflict. When you are first in love, the boxers left on the floor are just adorable. The heat turned up to 80 degrees is a darling idea. But eventually, familiarity breeds, if not contempt, plenty of irritation. Add to that the stresses of children, finances, and career—along with the real differences in the way men and women perceive the world—and it's a wonder any of us make it through the first few years of a relationship.

An intimate relationship itself is a living, breathing entity that must be nurtured and cared for daily, above our own individual needs or frustrations. It you want your relationship to work, you *both* must work at your relationship and care for it tenderly. It can't be one-sided, and it can't be neglected. We have to talk about what's bugging us, what we need from each other, and our dreams and disappointments. And we have to listen, really listen to what our beloved is saying so he or she feels heard and understood.

There is no doubt, your marriage or partnership is THE most valuable part of your life. If it's not, it should be. It should come before your work, hobbies, extended family, and—yes—even before your children. As a couple, you are the centerpiece of your family, and if the couple isn't strong, the family isn't strong. Both partners must be committed to putting the relationship as their top life priority. This commitment can't rest on empty words. It must be acknowledged between the two of you and demonstrated in your daily, even hourly, choices and actions to keep the relationship healthy and thriving.

To be good stewards of the relationship, we have to let go of personal needs long enough to heal the relationship before any rifts pull us apart. We can't allow communication to devolve into lashing out, stonewalling, or being right to protect our egos. By exercising some self-control, even when strong feelings make us want to say unspeakable things, we create a safe space for open communication, understanding, and deeper connection.

Says New York-based relationship therapist Harriet Pappenheim, LCSW, in an article on my blog, Live Bold and Bloom,

> Primarily, you need to become an expert on your partner. What makes your partner feel safe and secure, above all else? What will upset him/her? What will reassure that person?

> Try thinking back to the last time you had some sort of conflict or upset. How did your partner react? What would have soothed him/her? A

couple bubble can only exist between people who know each other really, really well. In time, each of you will come to know exactly how to comfort the other, in any kind of situation.

The most successful, intimate relationships involve proactive communication before a conflict ever arises. As stilted or awkward as it might seem, meeting with your spouse or partner on a regular basis to ask questions and learn about each other will protect your relationship from painful altercations, and, even better, it will create a new level of intimacy between you. I use probing questions regularly in my coaching practice to help clients uncover their deeper desires, needs, and fears. A strong question compels us to search within to find the answer, leading to profound moments of self-awareness and personal growth.

Within the context of a relationship, mutual questioning can provide these same benefits, and also allow each partner to participate in the awareness and growth of the other. More important, by mindfully listening to your partner without judgment or anger, you will understand more about his or her motivations, fears, pain, longings, and frustrations. You offer each other a safe space to be fully open and authentic, which ultimately draws you closer together and strengthens the bond of love between you.

How to Use These Questions

If you are reading this book alone, I strongly suggest you involve your partner and read the book together from the beginning. Make this a project the two of you undertake as a team. You both want to enter this work with the specific intention of strengthening and protecting your relationship, in addition to building intimacy and learning more about each other. These questions can be fun, humorous, enlightening, and deeply moving. You'll be surprised at how much more you discover about yourself and about each other.

You also will be challenged to make some personal changes in your behaviors, habits, and words. The questions will reveal unmet needs and behavior change requests from both of you. You will want to discuss these needs and requests and what you are each willing to change or accommodate for the other. There might be needs you can't fulfill or changes you're unwilling to make, and this will require honest and open discussion, so you can mutually arrive at alternative solutions.

There are 20 question topics in the book, each with ten or more related questions and question prompts. Consider working through the topics during the next 20 days, asking each other the questions from one topic per day. You can follow the order the topics are presented, or choose the topic

201 Relationship Questions

that feels most relevant to what's going on in your relationship at the time. If there are section topics that don't apply to you (for example, the section on parenting wouldn't apply if you don't have children), then feel free to skip over it. However, you still might find the questions and your partner's answers interesting and enlightening.

Both of you should keep a journal to make notes about your partner's responses and your own feelings after you complete the questions. You will also want to write down specific action steps both of you will take if a question prompts an adjustment in attitude, behavior, communication, or values.

When you begin a topic, you will each ask and answer the same question, taking turns as the first person to answer a question. It's often more difficult to be the first one to answer, as you might need time for your true feelings to bubble to the surface—or you might feel reticent to be fully open in your response. Also your partner's answers can influence your responses, so be mindful that your answers reflect your own true feelings and needs.

Your partner's answers or your own reactions might stimulate more questions or conversation between you, which can further develop connection and intimacy. Just be sure you listen intently to your partner's responses without interrupting or getting distracted. Sit close together as you are asking and answering, holding hands or touching. Even if your partner's answer makes you bristle or feel uncomfortable, try hard to simply listen without anger or judgment. Invite your partner to dig deeper and share more by asking, "Is there more?" once he or she answers the question. Keep asking this until your partner has nothing left to add.

Should a question provoke tension, pain, or anger between the two of you, try to ferret out the emotion behind the negative feelings. Ask your partner directly, "What is the emotion underneath your irritation? What was it about my response that made you feel upset?" In answering this, be careful not to project blame or criticism on your partner, even if you feel he or she is at fault. Speak about your inner feelings, which requires being vulnerable rather than defensive. You might say something like, "When you tell me you need more attention from me, it makes me feel like I'm not good enough and unappreciated for my efforts." When we acknowledge and understand the emotions behind our partner's anger or pain, it allows us to be more compassionate and willing to find workable solutions.

Should any of your discussions around these questions become too emotional or difficult to sort through without pain and anger, please seek the support of a trained relationship counselor to help you navigate the issue. Sometimes old wounds and pain from the past are too entrenched to unravel and heal without the help of a therapist. If this is the case, don't allow this emotional division to languish between you. Put your relationship first by seeking to treat and heal any fissures that could ultimately pull you apart or undermine the happiness of your connection.

One final note: I believe the physical environment in which you ask and answer these questions makes a big difference in how you respond and connect with each other. Don't undertake this important relationship work while kids are underfoot, dinner is cooking, or the TV is playing in the background. Choose a time when you know you won't be interrupted, perhaps early in the morning before anyone else awakens or in the evening during a quiet time.

Find a room in your home that feels peaceful and uncluttered without potential distractions or interruptions. Allow yourself an hour to finish all ten questions from one section and to discuss your feelings and reactions. Inform anyone else who lives in the house not to interrupt you during this hour. If necessary, leave the house to go to a quiet restaurant, sit somewhere in nature, or park the car somewhere in a peaceful setting. Consider this sacred time together that not only contributes to your happiness as a couple, but also makes you better parents, friends, and professionals. Your relationship happiness is the linchpin for happiness in all other areas of your life.

So, are you ready to get started?

Here are a few reminders:

- Grab your journals, and get a glass of water or a cup of tea (try to avoid alcohol as it alters your verbal self-control).

- Find your peaceful spot in the house or else-where.

- Flip a coin to see who will be the first one to answer the first question. Then alternate after that. Read the question and the information below the question out loud. Then ask the question again directly to your partner.

- Try not to read ahead to the next questions, but instead focus intently on the question you are asking and answering.

- Sit close to each other so you can touch and look at each other face to face.

- Give each other plenty of time to respond, and as you are listening to your partner an-swer a question, try not to think ahead about your own answers. Just be fully present for your partner and practice empathic listening skills. (See Resources for a blog article on these skills.)

At the end of each section, there is a follow-up prompt inviting you both to make behavior change requests of your partner. If your partner reveals a request for a change from you, discuss and write down specific actions steps you both intend to take and when you intend to take them. Making these changes can take time, as we need repetition and reinforcement to solidify new behaviors. Set up a system of gentle reminders and accountability for each other, and be patient as you both strive to be a better, more attentive, loving partner for the other.

Section 1: Feeling Loved

1. What specific behaviors and actions from me feel most loving to you?

Marriage counselor and author of *The 5 Love Languages*, Gary Chapman, believes there are five ways to express love emotionally. "Each person has a primary love language that we must learn to speak if we want that person to feel loved," says Chapman. These include words of affirmation, acts of service, receiving gifts, quality time, and physical touch. You can become aware of your love language by considering the actions and words from your partner that fill you with love and gratitude. Or you can notice your complaints to your partner, which reveal where you need more expressions of your love language.

2. How would you like me to verbally express my love?

If your love language is words of affirmation, verbal expressions are vital to feeling loved. But all of us need to hear words that are loving, tender, sexy, and affirming. Some people feel uncomfortable verbalizing their emotions, but real intimacy creates a safe bubble for the two of you to express your deepest feelings without fear or shame. You might both agree that fewer words are better for the two of you. If you differ here, it will require some compromise and stretching to accommodate each other.

3. What kind of physical touch feels the most loving?

Touch is our first sense to develop as babies, and it's the main way of showing love to a baby. We are wired to need touch. Physical affection is essential for the overall happiness and satisfaction of a romantic relationship. It solidifies our bonds as a couple. Studies have even shown that conflict is resolved more easily when there is more affection in the relationship. Some people need and desire more touch than others. In fact, one of you might be highly affectionate while the other requires less touch. Find out from each other the specific kinds of touch (hugging, holding hands, backrubs, etc.) that makes your partner feel loved and cherished.

4. What makes you feel more loving toward me?

Find out from each other the behaviors, words, and actions you each practice that elicit feelings of love and affection from your partner. Something as simple as a kind comment, a well-timed smile, or the way your partner makes a cup of coffee for you, can feel like the most generous, beautiful, or admirable gesture. It is often the small things that we appreciate most and that make us feel valued and treasured. Share these with each other, both to clarify them for yourself and to let your partner know what you appreciate about them.

5. How can I ask for more love from you?

There will be times when one or both of you don't feel loved as much you require or in the way you need to feel it. We want our partner to instinctively know what we need and to offer it without our having to ask. But that isn't always possible or realistic. As close as you might be as a couple, neither of you are mind readers. Sometimes you must ask for what you need. And it's good to ask in a way that is not judgmental, critical, or demeaning. Find out from your partner how you can ask for more love or a different expression of love in a way that inspires him or her to offer more.

6. What might I say or do that would feel unloving to you?

You both know the obvious words or actions that would feel unloving to your partner. Unkindness, criticism, dishonesty, and indifference will make anyone feel unloved and hurt. Sometimes we say or do things unknowingly that trigger pain and anger in our partner. Perhaps we trigger old wounds from the past or cross a boundary we didn't know existed. In an effort to keep peace, one partner might repress his or her feelings of hurt, but over time, keeping these feelings to oneself can cause resentment. Share with each other what your partner might do now or could do in the future to make you feel unloved.

7. How will I know when you need more love from me?

Sometimes we need more from our partner, but we aren't really clear what is making us feel unloved, neglected, or taken for granted. Or maybe we feel uncomfortable being direct, so we use passive-aggressive behaviors that reveal our pain or anger. We all turn to these behaviors from time to time to communicate our feelings—whether through pouting, withdrawal, or subtle comments. Examine your own behaviors in the past to see how you might be communicating your need for more love. Share these with your partner so they can recognize and identify them. Of course, direct communication is the best way to let your partner know you need more, but understanding these behaviors in each other opens the door for compassion and communication.

8. How often do you need to hear me say, "I love you"?

Those three little words are so powerful. For some people, hearing those words on a daily basis is as essential as water in a desert. A verbal expression of your partner's feelings makes you feel secure, acknowledged, and valued. Other people don't need to hear it as often. They know through their partner's actions and presence that they are loved. One of you might feel uncomfortable or silly saying the words regularly, while the other might sprinkle them throughout daily conversation. How often does your partner need to hear them from you? Be willing to offer these words as often as desired.

9. What does unconditional love mean to you?

Unconditional love is the ability to love the other person as he or she is in their essence. If you have fallen in love with this person and want to build a lasting relationship, then you must view him or her as a unique individual—not as an extension of yourself. But what does this mean in the dynamic of your particular relationship? How do you both view unconditional love, and how do you think it should be expressed within your marriage or connection?

10. How can we rekindle love when we see signs of apathy or distance?

Apathy and disconnection in the relationship can often creep up on a couple. When life gets busy with work, children, and other distractions, we might spend less time together, communicate less frequently, and feel anger or resentment that stifles intimacy. Maybe you are feeling some of this now. Even if you aren't, you need to protect your relationship from it. Work together to identify the first signs of distance between you, and talk about a plan for reconnecting should this happen.

Follow-up: Are there any behavior adjustments you'd like to request from your partner related to feeling loved? What specific action steps will you both take to help your partner feel more loved?

Write these down and determine how and when you will initiate these changes or actions.

Section 2: Respect and Kindness

11. What specific actions and words make you feel respected?

What is respect? According to the Oxford Dictionary, respect is "a feeling of deep admiration for someone or something elicited by their abilities, qualities, or achievements." When we are shown respect, we feel valued and acknowledged. We particularly want respect from the one person we love the most, whose opinion and regard are so deeply important to us. Feeling respected is different for every individual. What makes your partner feel respected might not mean as much to you. Talk to each other about where you need to feel respect and how your partner can best show you respect.

12. How have you been disrespected in the past, and how did it make you feel?

Part of understanding our own desires for respect derives from the ways we might have been disrespected in the past. If we are ignored, diminished, teased, or criticized for whom we are, what we value, or what we've achieved, we carry wounds that make us bristle when the behavior toward us is repeated even slightly. You can help yourself and your partner understand your need for respect by examining where you've lacked it in the past.

13. Am I doing anything now to make you feel disrespected?

Part of the discussion about respect needs to include any ways in which either of you might make your partner feel disrespected. This might be unconscious and perfectly innocent behavior, but if it causes your partner pain, you need to alter the behavior or language. Discuss this openly with each other and offer your partner a safe space to let you know about any feelings of being disrespected he or she might harbor.

14. Are there any ways in which you feel undeserving of respect?

We can unconsciously foster an attitude of disrespect from others when we don't respect ourselves or don't feel deserving of respect. You can send signals to others, including your spouse or partner, that you don't value yourself and therefore aren't worthy of their respect. Do you see yourself in this way? Often these feelings come from low self-esteem, or perhaps there is a valid reason you've lost respect for yourself. Your partner can offer you the compassion and love to safely reveal your feelings and discuss how to regain self-respect.

15. How can I support you in feeling more respected in this area?

When we lack self-esteem and self-respect in some area of our lives, it is immeasurably comforting and reassuring to have someone in our corner, willing to help us regain our footing. Sometimes it takes the tender care of our beloved to help us see our own worthiness. If your spouse or partner is lacking self-respect, find out how you can support efforts to rebuild and maintain it going forward.

16. What acts of kindness from me mean the most to you?

You've heard the saying, "It's the smalls things that count." Small acts of kindness often communicate the strongest expressions of love and respect. These small acts add up to make our partners feel appreciated and cherished. Find out from each other which acts of kindness are most valued. Find out if there are any small acts your partner would like from you that you haven't offered before.

17. How have I unknowingly been less than kind to you?

We might not mean to wound or neglect each other, but we can say or do things that cause our partner to bristle or feel pain. It's hard to hear that we might have unknowingly wounded our partners, but it's important to address these small paper cuts before they cause deeper wounds or resentments. Gently share any unkindness with each other, and discuss the reasons behind the pain or irritation.

18. How should I let you know that I feel you're being unkind?

Often unkind words or actions occur when we're tired, stressed, worried, or distracted. We all have those moments, no matter how hard we try to be loving and kind all the time. On those occasions, it's hard to be corrected or reminded of unkind behaviors. How would you like your spouse or partner to let you know you are acting in an unkind way or speaking unkindly so that you can avoid a conflict or defensive feelings?

19. Do you see me as a kind person to you and others?

Kindness is such an important trait to foster, not only toward your partner but also with anyone you encounter. It isn't hard to speak with kindness or to offer small acts of kindness daily. Unfortunately, in this busy, competitive, and demanding world, kindness isn't a highly regarded trait. We forget to be kind, because we aren't always rewarded for it. If you see the value of being kind and expressing it to others, and you want to be a kinder person, your spouse or partner can reflect back to you whether or not this is one of your strengths. If it's not, ask your partner how you could be more kind in general and how to develop this part of your personality.

20. What acts of kindness or service could we perform together that would strengthen our relationship?

It feels good to be kind to others, and if you value kindness as a couple, it provides another wellspring for intimacy and connection. Do you have a neighbor or friend who needs support? Is there a young person in your lives who could benefit from having you as mentors? Is there a cause or project that is meaningful to both of you? Talk about ways you can share in acts of kindness that would be fulfilling.

Follow-up: Are there any behavior adjustments you'd like to request from your partner related to respect and kindness? What specific action steps will you both take to help your partner feel more respect and kindness? Write these down and determine how and when you will initiate these changes or actions.

Section 3: Communication

21. How can we have more intimate conversations?

So often couples get in the habit of discussing the mundane and necessary topics related to running the house, raising the kids, and dealing with finances. The long, intimate conversations you had when you first fell in love get lost in the routines of daily life together. But it's these intimate conversations that create the strongest bonds between you and help you maintain closeness, romance, and trust. Discuss whether or not you are lacking in intimate conversations, and if so, how can you create the time to prioritize them?

22. What should I do if I need you to talk more to me?

Sometimes one partner in the relationship desires more intimate conversation than the other. One of you might want to talk, while the other needs time alone. Your partner might want to cuddle and talk after sex, and you might be ready to go to sleep. One of you might feel disconnected or in need of communication, while the other feels satisfied and fulfilled with the status quo. There is no right or wrong measure of intimate communication. Every couple must work this out together based on each partner's individual needs and desires. If you are the one who needs more communication, then you must communicate this to your partner. Define specifically what you need, and ask your partner what he or she is willing and able to do.

23. How can I let you know I don't feel like talking?

There will be times for both of you when you just don't want to have a deep or intimate conversation. You might be tired or stressed, or maybe you simply need time alone. This can feel like a rejection to your partner if he or she doesn't understand your withdrawal or refusal to connect. Discuss with each other how you can communicate your feelings without hurting or offending the other. Remember, neither of you can use these feelings as an excuse to avoid intimate communication altogether. A lack of close communication will eventually create a distance between you that is hard to repair.

24. How can I best communicate a problem or concern?

It's never pleasant to talk about conflict or difficulties, but they are inevitable in all relationships. Whether the problem relates to your relationship or it's a negative situation that impacts both of you, these difficult conversations provoke so many emotions. When we're caught up in the negative emotions, we can take it out on the messenger—in this case, your spouse or partner. Discuss together how you each react to hearing difficult information and how the other can present it so you both can discuss it with a clear head and kind words.

25. Is there anything about my tone of voice that bothers you?

So often it's not the words that are spoken but rather the way they are presented that causes us to be offended or wounded. Just a slight change in tone or inflection can spell the difference between a loving tease and biting sarcasm. The longer you live with someone, the better you recognize the nuances in your partner's verbal expressions. Sometimes these subtle vocal shifts are passive-aggressive ways of communicating irritation or frustration. Sometimes we aren't aware of how our tone might sound to others. Find out from your partner whether or not your tone of voice can be hurtful or offensive. How can you soften or change it to be more honest and kind?

26. What topics should we only discuss in person (not by text, email, or phone)?

Communication has changed drastically in the last decade or so. What was once only spoken in person is now spelled in abbreviated words and symbols on our smart phones. Feelings of love, anger, jealously, and desire are reduced to written words that can be misinterpreted or seem empty. There are some topics that need the interplay of voice, facial expression, touch, and setting. Intimate communication, relationship conflict, and important information simply can't be shared through electronic devices. They require face-to-face interaction. Talk together about the topics the two of you decide must be reserved for real time. Promise each other that you won't use email or texting as a platform for conflict or bitterness.

27. Do you feel completely free to talk with me about anything?

We all have secrets, regrets, past pain, and shameful feelings. We might repress these feelings and memories because they are so painful. But repressing them can lead to anxiety, depression, and unhealthy behaviors. If there is any place we should feel safe to share our pain and regret, it's with our intimate partner. Perhaps we hold back for fear of rejection or anger from our partner, but real intimacy can't happen if we don't feel safe in sharing and being vulnerable. We need to reassure our partners that their fears, shame, and pain will be treated with dignity and without judgment. We need to provide that safe space for them to know they are loved and accepted completely.

28. Am I free to talk with you about anything?

Sometimes our own past or old, entrenched beliefs make it difficult to discuss certain topics. Maybe it's uncomfortable to talk about your partner's sexual fantasies or to discuss differing religious beliefs. Maybe you don't like knowing about past relationships, or you get irritated listening to ongoing problems with a friend. Find out from your partner if there's anything he or she has a hard time discussing with you. Is it critical that your partner be your listening ear on this topic, or can you find support elsewhere? How can you reach a compromise or solution here?

29. What topics do you most enjoy discussing with me?

Intimate conversation is a wonderful way to learn more about each other. You can find areas of common interest and broaden your perspectives. Maybe you enjoy discussing books, movies, politics, or current events. Maybe you savor deep philosophical discussions or talking about self-improvement and personal growth. There might be topics you'd like to discuss with your partner that you haven't introduced yet. Ask each other what areas of conversation you'd like to develop.

30. How can I listen to you better so you feel completely heard?

Listening involves more than simply hearing the words of the other. Empathic, active listening means you give your full attention to your partner, without distractions or interruptions. It also involves reflecting back to you partner what you have heard them say. Ask your partner if they generally feel heard by you. If not, find out where you need to improve. You can learn more about empathic listening from an article on my blog (see Resources).

Follow-up: Are there any behavior adjustments you'd like to request from your partner related to communication? What specific action steps will you both take to help you both communicate better? Write these down and determine how and when you will initiate these changes or actions.

Section 4: Emotional Needs

31. What are your primary emotional needs?

Part of being human means having emotional needs. We want to be loved and to give live. We want to feel we belong and have a sense of purpose. We want to feel self-esteem and respect from others. These are some of the most common needs, but individuals have emotional needs unique to them. In a healthy relationship, both of you understand the other's primary emotional needs, and you both work to respond to them because you love and respect your partner. You can find a list of needs on my website to help you define your own (see Resources). Share your primary emotional needs with your partner.

32. Am I responsive enough to your emotional needs?

We can't expect any one person to meet all our emotional needs, even our love partners. Sometimes we have needs that are beyond the scope of any one person to handle. But we can ask our partners to be responsive to our needs and to honor them. There are some emotional needs your partner might be happy and willing to meet, but he or she is simply not aware of them. It's your job to enlighten your partner. There might be needs that they aren't able to meet. Discuss the emotional needs you have where you'd like more from your partner. Speak honestly and specifically about what you are each willing to offer the other, and discuss alternatives for getting your needs met without your partner if necessary.

33. What should I say to you when I need more from you emotionally?

It's hard to hear the words, "I need more from you. I need more love, more affection, more respect, and more intimacy." We all want to feel like we're enough, that we are appreciated and accepted for all that we do and give to our partners. But you can't intuit all your partner's needs, and you might not be able to understand or relate to some of them. Even so, your partner should feel comfortable expressing those needs and asking you to respond to them. How can you make that request safe and easy for your partner?

34. Do I give you enough emotional space?

One of your emotional needs might be autonomy and freedom. Perhaps you need less emotionally than your spouse does. Needing emotional space doesn't mean you don't want to be intimate or close with your partner. You can balance the need for closeness with the desire for space. Ask each other if you have enough emotional space. If not, exactly what kind of space do you need, and how can your partner support you in this need?

35. What could I do to make you feel more understood?

Even if we can't meet all of our partner's emotional needs, we can strive to empathize with him or her. We can listen and show we care. We can acknowledge the efforts at meeting his or her own needs (for self-esteem or independence, for example) or in reaching out to another support person to help. We can let our partners know they aren't in this alone, and that we acknowledge and understand their feelings and desires.

36. Do you feel free to express your emotions with me?

Some of us are more expressive with our feelings than others. We laugh and cry easily and have little difficulty saying what we feel. Others don't feel so free to express emotion, especially painful emotion. Or we might express our feelings in unhealthy ways, such as anger or withdrawal. In a love relationship, we need to feel safe expressing our deepest emotions, especially those that are painful or shameful. We need to know that our loved one will treat our feelings tenderly, without judgment or criticism. Find out from your partner whether or not he or she is completely at ease with you in expressing emotions. If not, what is holding him or her back?

37. Do you have any negative emotions about our relationship you need to express?

We might hold back when expressing our emotions because we fear the reaction of our partners. Maybe they will be hurt or angry. Maybe they won't understand. Maybe they'll diminish how we feel. If either of you are harboring negative emotions about the relationship, you need to discuss these and get to the root cause. When communicating negative emotions, speak kindly and constructively. When listening, set aside defensiveness. If negativity exists for one of you, it is an issue you both need to resolve.

38. What from your past has shaped your emotional needs and reactions?

So many of our emotional reactions and triggers are shaped by our childhood experiences. How you were parented and the environment in which you grew up can have a profound effect on your emotional well-being as an adult. Your significant other can't fully understand you and your needs until he or she knows something about how the past has shaped your outlook and behaviors. Share with each other the positive and negative events that have contributed to your particular emotional needs.

39. Would you consider yourself a highly sensitive person, and if so, how can I support you?

A highly sensitive person (HSP) is one who feels things more keenly than the average person. You notice more subtleties in the environment, feel overwhelmed by too much sensory input, and are easily affected by other people's moods. You have a rich inner life and enjoy creative pursuits. You also need time alone to recharge and get relief from too much stimulation. Highly sensitive people are extremely conscientious and try hard to please others. You can read more about highly sensitive people in my book, *Finely Tuned*. If one or both of you are highly sensitive, you will need to have a special understanding of the traits of HSPs and what they need in order to feel comfortable and thrive. This is particularly true for the non-sensitive, as many of the HSP traits might seem overly sensitive or needy. However, this trait is perfectly normal and has many positive qualities. Find out how your highly sensitive partner needs your understanding and support.

40. What other ways do you have for dealing with your emotions if I feel overwhelmed by

them?

When emotions run high during conflict or during times of difficulty or pain, both partners might be flooded with emotion and have little reserve to offer each other. If you are accustomed to turning to your spouse or partner for emotional support, then you need an alternative plan when you are both feeling overwhelmed. If one of you loses a job, there's a death in the family, or you have financial difficulties, you both might need outside support to see you through. What is your emotional back-up plan if your partner can't handle your emotions in a particular situation?

Follow-up: Are there any behavior adjustments you'd like to request from your partner related to emotional needs? What specific action steps will you both take to help you get your emotional needs met and to better understand the emotions of the other? Write these down and determine how and when you will initiate these changes or actions.

Section 5: Personal Boundaries

41. What should I never say to you in anger or playfulness?

There are some words or phrases that cross the threshold for acceptable language in your mind. Everyone has their own notion for what that threshold is. There might be playful name-calling that is perfectly fine, but other names that are deeply wounding. You might find certain words so ugly and demeaning that you simply don't want to hear them, even in jest—but especially in anger. You both might agree that you'll never yell the words, "I hate you" or "Maybe we should divorce," in the heat of anger. Discuss these out-of-bounds words and phrases and honor each other's requests related to them.

42. Have you shared all your personal boundaries with me? If not, what are they?

Personal boundaries are the imaginary lines we draw around ourselves to maintain balance and protect our bodies, minds, emotions, and time from the behavior or demands of others. If you tend to be a people pleaser, you might allow your partner to unknowingly cross your boundaries. In order for your spouse to honor your boundaries, you must be aware of them yourself and communicate them fully and freely. Find out from each other what personal boundaries are important to each of you. You can read more about personal boundaries in a post on my website (see Resources).

43. Is there anything I do now that crosses your boundaries and makes you uncomfortable?

If you aren't aware of your own personal boundaries, you might not be able to answer this question without some thought. Sometimes we're aware of a vague sense of unease or irritation in our relationship, but we aren't sure why we feel this way. Often it's because our partner is doing something to cross a personal boundary. This might relate to sex, interruptions of time, expectations, or privacy needs, for example. Find out from your partner how you might be stepping over the line and how you can adjust your behavior or words to prevent resentment and frustration.

44. In what ways do you see me as a unique individual, separate and apart from our relationship?

Before you were a couple, you were each individuals with your own sense of self and personal identity. As a couple, you have created a unified identity, but that doesn't mean you should lose your individuality. Each partner should respect and value the other as a separate, unique person, not merely an extension of the relationship. By viewing your partner as his or her own person, you are validating him or her and reinforcing all the reasons you fell in love.

45. Do you feel free to be yourself and express yourself with me? If not, why?

We can lose part of our personal identity when we enter into an intimate relationship. Sometimes this happens because we look to the other person to help define us. It can also happen when one partner is more dominant and the other accommodates or acquiesces in order to maintain peace. If you aren't free or willing to be yourself and express yourself, not only are you compromising your self-esteem but also you're denying your partner the opportunity to know you fully and completely. Invite your partner to be fully authentic and open, and be willing to listen to any role you might play in his or her reticence to be completely authentic.

46. Is there anything about our sexual intimacy that makes you unhappy or uncomfortable? If so, what?

It can be difficult to openly discuss differences in sexual desires or needs, especially if you aren't comfortable with something your partner is doing or saying during sex, or you have differing sex drives. If you aren't compatible sexually, it can undermine intimacy in your relationship in general, especially if you don't address it. By discussing your sexual desires and wishes, you both can find a middle ground that feels acceptable and comfortable. Each of you might need to compromise at times in order to meet the needs of the other. Allow your love for each other to be the guiding force as you seek to create a satisfying and comfortable sex life.

47. Are there any physical possessions or spaces in our home that you'd like to have as your own?

Couples often create the pattern of "what's yours is mine, and what's mine is yours." If you live together, you will share many possessions and physical spaces in your home. However, you might have possessions you don't want to release as a "couple item." Maybe it's your laptop or a favorite coffee mug. Maybe you don't want to share your razor or give up your pillow. This need can extend to spaces in your home. One or both of you might need a personal "sanctuary" that's all your own. Being married or living together doesn't require you to share everything or drop the courtesy of asking before borrowing. Discuss together any boundaries around possessions and spaces in your home you'd like to reinforce or implement.

48. Do you ever feel uncomfortable saying "no" or speaking up for yourself with me? If so, why?

Healthy self-esteem requires we feel confident speaking up for ourselves, even if it feels uncomfortable or creates conflict. Sometimes it's just easier to go along rather than saying, "No, I don't want to do that." There are times to keep the peace, but if it becomes your fallback position, you're creating an unhealthy imbalance in your relationship. You undermine your partner's respect for you, and you diminish your own self-esteem. If you're the partner who always seems to get his or her way, you are equally responsible for establishing balance by getting to the root of the issue. Find out why your loved one isn't saying what he or she means and discuss how you both can correct the problem.

49. Where are you unwilling to compromise?

Some amount of compromise is essential for the happiness and longevity of close relationships. But as unique individuals, you have values, goals, and standards you simply can't compromise. Maybe one of you feels strongly about his or her faith, but the other doesn't share the same beliefs. You might be a committed vegetarian, but your partner isn't willing to give up eating meat. Both of you can have values and ideals you are unwilling to compromise and still remain a strong and happy couple—as long as you each respect and honor the other's feelings.

50. How should we handle it, if a boundary has been crossed?

Awareness of each other's boundaries goes a long way in building a respectful and loving dynamic in which you both desire to honor the needs of the other. However, it's inevitable you will cross each other's boundaries from time to time. We are imperfect and forgetful and can get caught up in our own needs. To minimize potential conflict over boundary issues, create a proactive plan for how you will handle it when one of you steps over the comfort line with the other. Humor goes a long way in deflecting irritation and defensiveness. Perhaps you can create a funny line or cue to gently remind each other of your boundaries.

Follow-up: Are there any behavior adjustments you'd like to request from your partner related to your personal boundaries? What specific action steps will you both take to help establish and honor boundaries? Write these down and determine how and when you will initiate these changes or actions.

Section 6: Sex and Affection

51. How often would you like to have sex?

Sex is an important way to express your love and desire for each other. According to David Schnarch, PhD, in an article on the site EverydayFamily.com, "I believe that sex matters: It's the glue that keeps us together and, without it, couples become 'good friends' at best, or 'bickering roommates' at worst." The two of you might have differing opinions on the frequency of sex, but Dr. Schnarch suggests at least once a week to maintain your close connection. Talk with each other about your life demands, stresses, and emotions that interfere with your sex life. Come to an agreement about the minimum amount of sex that is acceptable for your relationship.

52. What sexual fantasies do you have that we can enjoy together?

Don't allow your intimate life to fall into a rut—the same position, the same day of the week, the same room. If sex becomes boring, you'll be less inclined to initiate or respond. Maybe you feel shy about discussing your fantasies with your partner, especially if they are particularly, um, progressive. If you have a deep level of trust and respect between you, having this conversation could enhance your relationship. Take it slow and present your fantasies gradually so your partner isn't put off. Simply talking about your fantasies can be a way to spice up your relationship.

53. How could we improve our sex life?

Beyond frequency and fantasy, what could you do to make your sex life more intimate, exciting, and fun? Daily obligations, stress, and exhaustion can make sex feel obligatory and routine. We fall into a rut and lose touch with the creativity, romance, and desire we had early in the relationship. Talk together about how to improve your sex life. This might include changes in your schedules and behavior. It might mean changing locations, positions, or timing. You might brainstorm creative ideas for using toys, watching movies, or wearing sexy clothing. View this conversation as a creative project you work on together.

54. Do you feel comfortable talking with me about your sexual needs? If not, why?

One of you might not feel completely comfortable discussing sexual needs and desires. If you were raised in a household where sex was never discussed, or it was seen as shameful or embarrassing, you might feel reticent to talk about it or share your inner feelings. Or you might fear your partner won't react positively to your needs and desires. Both of you need to feel safe discussing sex, but you also need to respect each other's sexual histories and issues that might contribute to negative or shameful feelings around sex. What seems fun and exciting to one of you might feel sordid and unnatural for the other. Find out from your partner the reasons behind any discomfort discussing sexual needs. Offer him or her a safe space to discuss feelings and to share anything he or she has previously felt reticent to discuss.

55. How much foreplay before sex is important to you?

Foreplay serves a physical and emotional purpose in helping a couple prepare for a mutually satisfying sexual encounter. Women in particular need foreplay, because it takes women a longer time to reach the state of arousal that leads to orgasm. Beyond the physical importance of foreplay, it communicates that you both want to offer the time and attention couples need for intimate lovemaking. You might differ in how much foreplay you desire, so discuss your needs and how you can reach a meeting of the minds and bodies.

56. How can I make you feel more desirable and sexy?

A huge part of feeling sexually confident and happy is knowing you are desirable and sexy in the eyes of your spouse or partner. When we don't feel our partner really desires us sexually, it undermines the intimacy of the sexual encounter for both partners. You might need to hear your partner tell you that you look hot and sexy, or you might need to see it in the facial expressions. Maybe you'd like words of affirmation about your desirability in between sexual encounters, or you'd like your partner to surprise you with sexual overtures because he or she simple "can't resist you." Find out exactly what your partner needs from you to feel sexy.

57. How much non-sexual affection would you like?

Non-sexual affection—like hugging, backrubs, snuggling, hand-holding, and massage—is an essential part of emotional intimacy between you and your partner. Touch bonds the two of you as a couple and creates a closer connection. Physical affection can lead to sex, but that shouldn't be the goal of initiating it. Affection should be shared as a way of showing love and reinforcing the desire to be physically close to your partner. Women tend to need and desire more non-sexual affection than men, but both men and women benefit from the effects of physical closeness.

58. What kind of affection feels loving and good to you?

You might love a backrub, but your partner finds it uncomfortable. She might want to snuggle in bed before sleep, but you might need your space. All affection isn't equal, and what feels loving and re-laxing to one of you might not be your spouse's cup of tea. Talk together about the expressions of phys-ical affection that you like the most and how you can reciprocate with affectionate touch that your spouse enjoys.

59. How much affection in public are you comfortable with?

You might be comfortable kissing, hugging, and snuggling in the privacy of your home, but when you're with other people, it makes you feel awkward. He might pull you onto his lap at home, and it makes you feel loved and desired. But when it happens in public, you feel embarrassed. How much affection is too much in public settings? Discuss the middle ground where you both feel comfortable and happy touching when others are around.

60. When do you need affection the most?

Some of us welcome and need affection when we're feeling down or going through a life difficulty. We might require it after a fight with our spouse as a way of solidifying reconciliation. If we feel sick or tired, we long for a loving touch. But others feel less inclined to give or receive affection during these times. There are times affection is simply a way of connecting, and other times when it can be deeply healing. Discover the occasions when affection is most meaningful to your partner.

Follow-up: Are there any behavior adjustments you'd like to request from your partner related to your sex life? What specific action steps will you both take to help enhance your sex life? Write these down and determine how and when you will initiate these changes or actions.

Section 7: Emotional Intimacy

61. What activities and interests can we develop that will bring us closer?

Closeness develops between a couple when you spend time together doing things that are fun and enjoyable. You might not share all the same interests, but you can develop some mutual interests that you enjoy together. According to many psychologists, reading together, even reading different books, can bring partners closer together. But any fun activity you can share that involves cooperation and shared experience will tighten your bond. Fun and play are the antidotes for boredom and disconnection. Brainstorm together some mutual interests or new activities you can try. See Resources for a link to ideas for summer and winter fun activities.

62. What could I do that would cause you to pull away from me?

To feel close with your partner, you need to feel safe and respected. You need a protective bubble around your relationship that binds the two of you together as a team—in friendship, physical intimacy, and companionship. When one of you pulls away, the bubble is compromised and the relationship is in danger of losing its strong bond. We can pull away from each other briefly, but if the distance grows too vast without repair, the damage can be serious. Before this happens, learn from each other what might cause the other to pull away. Do either of you have behaviors or use words that push the other away?

63. Who do we know that has the kind of intimacy we want?

Emotional intimacy might not be something you've consciously considered before. Perhaps you think closeness as a couple is something that should always be there. Maybe you don't realize how much closer you could be if you just changed some behaviors and attitudes. Think about couples you know who seem to be close and happy with each other. What do they have in their relationship that you'd like to have? What could both of you do to foster that connection?

64. When do you feel the most connected to me?

There are times when we feel extremely close and connected with our partners. Maybe it's something they say or a kindness they offer. It could be as simple as time sitting together and talking or taking a walk together. Your spouse might not know how he or she is pulling you closer, so share with each other the ways in which you feel especially close and what your partner does to foster that. You might both surprise each other.

65. What are the life lessons I can learn from you?

Our love relationship is the main setting for our own personal growth. Through this relationship, we learn compromise, teamwork, empathy, compassion, resilience, patience, and commitment. But we also have the opportunity to expand simply by viewing our partner as a teacher. What life experiences and mindsets does your partner have that can enlighten you? What are his or her strengths that you can adopt? How does his or her worldview reflect a possible new way of thinking for you? Discuss with each other what lessons you can share and what you have learned from your partner.

66. What kind of memories do we want to create

together?

A lifetime of memories are the fabric of a happy, intimate relationship. When you look back on your life together over the next few years and into old age, what do you want to be able to say about it? What kind of life can you create right now that will serve as the source of happy, positive memories in the future? This might involve special time with children, family, and friends, in addition to travel, shared activities, adventure, and romance. As poet Mary Oliver asks in her poem "The Summer Day" —"Tell me, what is it you plan to do with your one wild and precious life?"

67. What will be the early warning signs that our relationship is in trouble?

A loss of closeness and intimacy is a huge red flag that the relationship is on the skids. But what does that mean for your particular relationship? Every couple is different in how they feel close and the specific actions and words that maintain that close-ness. Before either of you unconsciously allow the connection to weaken, be proactive in knowing what to watch out for. Each of you might have dif-fering warning signals, so be sure you both com-municate what spells potential trouble on the hori-zon. More important, when you sense something is off, be sure you open the lines of communication with your spouse. Don't allow problems to simmer.

68. What do you think makes our relationship special?

When you first fall in love, it feels like you're the only couple in the world who has such an amazing connection. You see yourselves as uniquely matched and protected from the conflict and drama you witness in other couples around you. As time goes on, some of the initial enthrallment wears off, and you begin to see each other and your relationship more realistically, especially in times of stress, conflict, or boredom. However, by mentally revisiting those early days and reminding yourselves of what made you unique and special as a couple, you can reignite those romantic feelings and strengthen your emotional bond.

69. What are your deepest dreams and desires for yourself and for us?

The ability to share your innermost feelings with your partner is one of the most valuable ways we create intimacy. We all have hopes and dreams, for ourselves and our relationships, and we need to express these with the one person who can help us realize them. Sometimes our dreams and goals can feel threatening to our partner. Maybe one of you wants to change jobs or move to a different city. Part of intimacy requires that in sharing your dreams, you listen to your partner's fears and concerns. In listening to your partner's dreams, you allow him or her the freedom to share without immediately undermining the person.

70. What should we do if we start to lose our emotional closeness?

Marriage therapists often suggest you should increase the amount of time together when emotional intimacy is damaged. This is important, but if you are having a lot of conflict or feel distanced, it might be difficult to enjoy time together. Discussing and resolving the reasons behind conflict can help you reconnect. Busyness is a common reason for disconnection. Too much time spent with kids, work, and other distractions can pull you apart and make one or both of you feel unloved. It's not just the time together that counts, but rather how you spend the time in ways that foster rebuilding intimacy and trust. What are some specific actions you both commit to taking if you begin to pull apart?

Follow-up: Are there any behavior adjustments you'd like to request from your partner related to emotional intimacy? What specific action steps will you both take to help enhance your closeness and connection? Write these down and determine how and when you will initiate these changes or actions.

Section 8: Personal Habits

71. Do I have any personal habits that get on your nerves? If so, what are they?

Whether it's leaving clothes on the floor or forgetting to put the lid down, we all have habits that can be irritating. Most of these habits are benign, but it's these little things that can add up to bigger conflict. In sharing these habit frustrations with each other, be aware that most of our personal habits are unconscious, not intentional. Be gentle and understanding in asking for a behavior change and in reminding your partner when he or she forgets.

72. How should I let you know about a habit of yours that bothers me?

Rather than nagging or getting frustrated, you can find out how your spouse would prefer to be reminded or made aware of an irritating habit. Humor often diffuses the frustration, but sometimes a single word or kind request is all it takes. Discuss together how each of you can avoid reacting defensively or passive-aggressively to a request to address a personal habit.

73. Do you have any bad habits you feel you must hide from me?

If you smoke, drink more than you should, take recreational drugs, or have any other habit you know would upset your partner, you might feel the need to hide this from him or her. Hiding this from your partner is not only stressful for you, but also it can seriously damage the trust and intimacy in your relationship. Now is the time to come clean and to ask for support from your spouse in revising this habit. If you are the partner hearing about this habit for the first time, try to understand and be kind. This situation might require the support of a professional relationship therapist.

74. What positive habits could we work on together?

Discuss together goals you each have related to health, fitness, productivity, mental health, personal growth, learning, etc. Working together to build positive habits will make it more fun and provide built-in motivation and accountability. Having a common goal also strengthens the bonds of your relationship. You can learn more about the skills of creating sustainable habits by reading my website article listed in the Resources.

75. What bad relationship habits have we developed that need to change?

As we become more comfortable and settled with

each other, it's easy to fall into bad habits that don't serve the health of the relationship. Maybe you automatically watch too much TV rather than talking or neglect to say "thank you" to each other. Maybe you've settled into routines that are separate, rather than seeking time together. Discuss these bad habits and what you both need to do to change them.

76. What parenting habits have we developed that negatively impact our relationship?

If you have children, it's easy to allow them to become the center of your attention and time. When you put your children ahead of your relationship together, you are actually doing a disservice both to your children and your marriage. Allowing children to stay up past bedtimes, interrupt your conversations, or demand your time in other ways takes time away from your adult interactions with your partner or spouse. How do you both need to change your parenting habits so you can improve your connection and provide better boundaries and structure for your kids?

77. How are we positive role models for our children, family, or friends with our habits?

Your habits and behaviors reflect to the world what's important to you and what kind of couple you are. Are you choosing to be positive role models to the people important to you through your habits? What messages do you both want to send to the world by the habit choices you make together and separately?

78. Do I have emotional habits that drag you down or make you feel bad? If so, what are they?

It's easy to get stuck in thinking and emotional habits that are self-defeating and negative. The longer we allow negative, looping thoughts to have free reign in our minds, the more entrenched these thoughts become. These thoughts lead to feelings of anxiety, depression, and anger. Sometimes we can't see this pattern in ourselves, but the person closest to us is the daily witness to our emotional and mental habits—and he or she can become infected by them. How could you be infecting the one you love with your emotional habits, and what can you do to break the cycle? Find additional tips for changing your mental attitude in my website article listed in the Resources.

79. Are you comfortable with my hygiene and self-care? If not, what makes you uncomfortable?

When we first fall in love, we do everything we can

to put our best foot forward with our appearance and hygiene. As we get more comfortable in the relationship, we also feel more comfortable "letting our hair down" and letting some things go. It's hard to tell your loved one that you're offended or uncomfortable with some aspect of his or her personal care. However, if it's undermining your sexual desire, affection, or respect for your spouse, it needs to be addressed in a kind and loving way.

80. How can we be more accepting of areas of incompatibility with our habits?

There will be some personal habits one or both of you are unwilling to change. You can't be completely compatible in all your behaviors, and each of you need to feel the freedom to have independent habits that are important to you. Maybe you've always read before bed, but your spouse wants you turn out the light. You might love playing video games, even if your partner finds it a waste of time. Discuss together how you both can be accepting and respectful of these areas of incompatibility. Go one step further, and invite your spouse to join you in your habit to see if he or she might enjoy it on occasion.

Follow-up: Are there any behavior adjustments you'd like to request from your partner related to personal habits? What specific action steps will you both take to improve your habits together and change habits that need changing? Write these down and determine how and when you will initiate these changes or actions.

Section 9: Disagreements and Differences

81. What do I say or do that really pushes your buttons?

"All she needs to do is use that one tone of voice, and my blood starts to boil." "When he rolls his eyes at me, I want to tear my hair out." These button-pushing situations are common in all relationships, whether they are done intentionally or not. We probably know some of the things that make our partner bristle, and maybe we try to push those buttons from time to time. But there might be words or actions you each use unknowingly that have the same effect. Kindly share these with each other and offer the reasons why you get hurt or offended. Understanding helps foster compassion and motivation to change.

82. What seems to be the recurring theme or themes in our conflict?

Often couples find they argue about the same things repeatedly. The arguments might take on a different form, but the substance is generally the same. They get caught in a cycle of negative engagement without ever coming to any satisfying resolution or compromise to break free of the pattern. By allowing this same conflict to go on and on, you aren't putting the relationship first. You are allowing it to languish with an unsettled divide between you. Talk about these recurring conflict themes. What can you do to resolve them once and for all?

83. What makes you feel heard and understood when we have conflict?

During conflict, it's difficult not to react and get angry or bitter. We find ourselves saying unkind things, being passive-aggressive, or trying to intimidate or wound our partner in an effort to protect ourselves. When disagreements occur, the most important thing you can do is to work together to rebuild the connection between you. That requires self-control and mutual understanding. You both need to feel heard and understood before you can reach a resolution or compromise. Find out what makes your partner feel that you truly hear and understand his or her position and what he or she is trying to communicate.

84. When is the best time for us to resolve conflict?

You're out to dinner, and you've both had a few cocktails. One of you says something sarcastic, and the other responds in kind. Before you know it, you're fighting under your breath, as onlookers nearby feel the tension pulsating from your table in waves. Not the best place to work out a problem, right? Neither is the family dinner table, just before you turn the light out for sleep, or as one of you is heading out the door to work. Conflict might arise spontaneously, but you should both agree to resolve it at a time when you are both calm, free of distractions, and not under the influence of alcohol or drugs. The sooner you can resolve a problem, the better, but the timing of your conversation is key to reaching a positive result for both of you. Determine together the best time for these conflict resolution discussions.

85. How can you best manage anger or frustration so we can talk calmly?

There's no question that it's hard to remain calm and even-tempered when you feel angry, hurt, or frustrated. But these feelings cloud your ability to work together toward resolution. You're likely to say or do something that will only make the situation worse. If you have a problem containing your feelings in the heat of the moment, what can you do to restore emotional equilibrium to a place where you can have a calm discussion?

86. What do you see as the major differences between us in the way we handle conflict?

Everyone has learned different ways for handling conflict. It's been modeled by our parents and other role models, and, in part, it's reflective of our personality type and level of confidence and self-esteem. One of you might retreat and withdraw during conflict, while the other yells and screams. Neither reaction is healthy or productive. What is your typical "conflict style" and how does it differ from your spouse's?

87. Which of these differences do we need to work on for healing, resolving, or managing?

If you have differing conflict styles, you need to determine a new way that works for both of you. One of you might need to agree stop raising her voice and the other needs to be fully present in the discussion rather than clamming up. Talk about your differing styles with the main goal of maintaining the integrity of your relationship. How do you both need to modify the way you approach conflict so your partner doesn't feel put off?

88. What should we do if we reach an impasse?

There will likely be times in the life of your relationship that you simply can't resolve an issue. You can't reach a compromise, and neither of you is willing to back down or let go. You can't allow this impasse to remain untended. Whether you decide to find a mediator, go to counseling, or draw straws, you need a plan in place for these impasse situations.

89. What can we promise each other that we will never say or do during times of conflict?

"Maybe we should just split up." "I never really loved you in the first place." "I can't talk to you. I'm leaving." There are some words so hurtful or demeaning, you regret them the minute they leave your mouth. Or you can do something so childish or thoughtless, it leaves an indelible wound on your spouse. Find out from each other what those "line crossing" words and behaviors are, and make a pact that you will avoid them at all costs. Consider putting this in writing, as it strengthens your personal commitment to each other.

90. How can we reframe conflict to make it a positive opportunity or experience for us?

Healthy couples view conflict not so much as an opportunity to get one's way or blow off steam, but rather as an opportunity for growth and learning. What can you learn about yourself during times of conflict? How can both of you grow as individuals and as a couple? How does conflict resolution help you in other areas of your life together and apart?

Follow-up: Are there any behavior adjustments you'd like to request from your partner related to disagreements and differences? What specific action steps will you both take to improve your conflict resolution and understanding of each other during conflict? Write these down and determine how and when you will initiate these changes or actions.

Section 10: Past Wounds

91. What are your deepest wounds from the past and how can I support you there?

Our childhood experiences and relationships with our parents and siblings can create emotional wounds we carry into adulthood. If you suffered loss, abuse, neglect, or tragedy in your youth, you will have scars that likely impact your relationship. Having the support and compassion of the one person you love most can provide much needed healing and comfort. But you must be willing to share these past wounds with your loved one and understand how they impact your emotions and behaviors as an adult. Your partner needs to know how he or she can best provide the support you need.

92. What pain or wounds from past relationships might be impacting our relationship?

Past love relationships can also impact our self-esteem and confidence, especially if the relationship ended badly. We learn many positive lessons from past loves, but we can also carry over insecurities, anger, resentment, and fears. We might hold back from emotional intimacy for fear of getting hurt again. It's hard to be vulnerable and share these old wounds with your partner, but, in sharing, you open yourself to loving fully again and finding the safe refuge for being fully yourself. Discuss together how these past relationship issues might be causing misunderstandings or conflict, and what both of you can do to mitigate this.

93. How have your parents and their relationship impacted your expectations or needs in our relationship?

Our first role models in love, relationships, and conflict resolution are our parents. If they had a happy, emotionally mature marriage, then we had positive role models teaching us how to choose a loving partner and how to speak and behave within a committed relationship. However, if our parents were unhappy and fought constantly, or if we were raised by a single parent, we didn't benefit from that positive modeling. Instead, we might have picked up immature, self-defeating, or divisive behaviors that simply can't work in a good relationship. This requires we learn from scratch how to be in a healthy relationship. Talk together about your parents' relationships and how they influenced you for good or bad.

94. What emotional patterns do you see yourself repeating?

Just as we tend to have conflict patterns in our love relationship, as individuals we have emotional patterns or habits we tend to repeat unconsciously. Maybe we find ourselves feeling insecure regularly, or we tend to be easily angered over trivial things. Sometimes we can get trapped in negative, looping thoughts that pull us into anxiety or depression. These patterns can impact the quality of your love relationship if they aren't addressed. When you're preoccupied with your own pain and unhappiness, you can't be available for your partner. Discuss these emotional patterns with each other, and how they might be impacting your spouse. What actions can you take to address these patterns?

95. What do I unconsciously do that triggers pain from the past?

Because you and your partner are so close, he or she is the person most apt to trigger past pain.

Maybe your father was verbally abusive, so any raised voice makes you tremble with anxiety. Perhaps your mom was sick in bed for a long time before she died, so any time your wife gets sick, you feel scared and resentful. Sometimes it's hard to identify the past event that your partner's actions or words are triggering, but if you ponder it, you'll likely see the thread of connection. Talk about this with each other and share what your spouse might be doing to trigger your pain.

96. How can I make you feel safe to be vulnerable about your pain and fears?

Sharing your inner pain and fears is really difficult. You might fear your partner will reject you if he or she knows the "truth" about your past, or you might not want to relive the pain. Maybe you feel you can just sweep it under the rug, and it will all go away. But past pain has a way of showing up in the most unpredictable ways—from depression to rage. You need a healthy, supportive outlet for sharing your deepest fears and wounds, and your partner needs to hear how to make you feel safe to share.

97. Is there anything in your past you are uncomfortable sharing with me, and if so, how can I make you feel more comfortable?

You might be reticent to share a situation from the

past because of something your partner has said or done that makes you feel judged or insecure. Maybe you had an abortion as a teenager, but your husband thinks abortion is wrong. Or perhaps you treated a past girlfriend badly, but you fear sharing your regret about it because you don't want your wife to know you acted this way. If you're holding on to a secret or past event you know you should share with your spouse, but you don't feel comfortable, tell your spouse why you're uncomfortable and afraid to share, and ask for his or her understanding and support. You might need the help of a counselor to navigate this if you find it too difficult.

98. How are you allowing the past to continue to make you unhappy?

The past has a way of creeping up on us and infecting our happiness with bitterness, shame, and regret. This happens to everyone to some degree or another, and it takes awareness and conscious action to prevent the past from overwhelming your present-day happiness. Ask yourself and your partner how the past might contribute to any unhappiness between you or as individuals. Don't allow past pain to harm your intimacy and connection.

99. What steps are you willing to take to heal from the past?

If you allow the past to make you unhappy without doing anything about it, you're facilitating the deterioration of your relationship. A couple can't survive happily if one partner is stuck with emotional baggage he or she can't release. It takes willingness and determination to heal, but it is possible with support from a professional. Ask your spouse if he or she is willing to take the steps necessary to move beyond the past so your relationship can thrive.

100. What can we both learn from our past wounds that will help us improve our relationship going forward?

All of this discussion about the past and old wounds might seem unnecessary and painful, but it's important to air it out so you can move on. Before you leave past pain behind, take a few minutes to talk about what you've learned from it and how you can apply what you've learned to your relationship growth. Express gratitude for all your experiences, good and bad, and discuss how these challenges have made you both stronger as individuals and as a couple.

Follow-up: Are there any behavior adjustments you'd like to request from your partner related to past wounds? What specific action steps will you both take to improve your compassion and understanding of each other and yourselves related to the past? Write these down and determine how and when you will initiate these changes or actions.

Section 11: Time Together and Alone

101. How much time do you think is optimal for us to spend together as a couple?

Our time together as a couple is often dictated by the other demands in our lives—work, children, and the basic tasks of daily life. Sometimes we allow these demands to encroach on time we should devote to spending with our partner. One of you might desire more "together time" than the other, or you both might enjoy time alone and neglect to reconnect as often as you should in order to maintain close communication and intimacy. Discuss together the ideal amount of time you'd like to spend together, and what is getting in the way of your spending time together.

102. On a typical day, how would you like us to spend time together?

Have either of you taken the time to consider how you want to be together as part of your regular routine? Do you wake up and rush out the door, or do you enjoy a cup of coffee together in morning? Do you make time to talk on the phone during the day? Do you carve out time in the evenings, even when it's hectic, to reconnect and share the details of your day? Discuss together how each of you would like to spend time as a couple during the day and what needs to change in order to make that happen.

103. How much time do we need to spend talking about our relationship?

If you are working through this book together, you are spending a lot of concentrated time talking about your relationship. But once you finish this process, how often do you want to discuss the health and joy of your relationship? Discuss how often you want to check in with each other to work through issues, discuss your relationship goals, and define ways to strengthen your relationship.

104. How much time is optimal for us to spend going out and having fun?

A vital part of intimacy is shared fun. The two of you need to connect in joy and play rather than focusing on serious or day-to-day matters constantly. Discuss what each of you considers to be fun activities, either at home or outside of the house, and how often you want to enjoy these activities. You might differ on what you find fun, but create a system to accommodate each other so you show your partner you're willing to step out of your comfort zone.

105. How much alone time do you need?

One of you might be an introvert or highly sensitive person and require more time alone in order to recharge or regain emotional balance. Introverts tend to crave more time alone than extraverts, so if you are a "mixed" couple, discuss the unique needs each of you might have related to togetherness. How can you find balance in the relationship so you both get your needs met for time alone and together? Understanding why your partner needs time alone can help both of you feel better about being apart when necessary.

106. What triggers you to crave time alone?

Sometimes we need time alone for creative think-ing, brainstorming, problem solving, or to calm down after conflict. If we've been driving in traffic or have spent a long day tending to children, we might need time to ourselves to relax. Each of you likely has certain triggers than make you want to be alone. Share these with each other so you both un-derstand when and why your partner might need a break.

107. How can I let you know I need alone time without hurting your feelings?

When your spouse disappears and closes the door or decides to go for a walk without you, it can feel like a rejection. Even the closest couples need time away from their partner, but it's often hard to com-municate this need for fear of wounding the person you love. Discuss how you can communicate your need for alone time in a way that doesn't trigger hurt feelings.

108. If we differ on the amount of time we need alone, how can we compromise?

You might need an hour after work by yourself to decompress, while your partner craves some time with you to talk and share the events of the day.

What do you do? How do you both get your needs met without one or the other feeling like they are giving up something important? Brainstorm ways you can work through these specific differences so that it's a win-win for both of you.

109. How are we allowing our children, work, or other distractions or commitments to compromise our time together?

In order to really spend quality time together, you must prioritize this special time. You can't allow other people or distractions to pull you away from each other. Does this happen in your relationship? How are these interruptions compromising your time as a couple? Discuss the most common disruptions you've been allowing to creep in to your sacred time together.

110. What are some specific actions we can take so we can enjoy more time together?

Now that you know what has been pulling you apart or interrupting your time together, think of ways you can correct or change these situations. Do you need to create new rules for your children? Can you turn off phones, computers, and other electronic distractions? Do you need to leave the house so you aren't tempted to work on tasks or housekeeping? Write down any ideas you might have and how you plan to implement them.

Follow-up: Are there any behavior adjustments you'd like to request from your partner related to spending time together or being alone? What specific action steps will you both take to improve your quality time together and understanding of each other and yourselves related to your needs for alone time? Write these down and determine how and when you will initiate these changes or actions.

Section 12: Friends

111. How much time do you want to spend with your friends?

Friendships for both of you are an important part of living a full and joyful life. Both of you likely have friends you developed prior to becoming a couple and friends you've created in individual pursuits through work, sports, hobbies, or elsewhere. It's important to maintain these friendships and to feel free to spend individual time with your friends. Sometimes a partner might feel jealous or frustrated by the amount of time you spend socializing with friends. Find out from each other how much time you desire to be with your friends without your partner.

112. How should we handle it, if one of us feels resentful of time spent with friends?

One of you might have more friends or enjoy more time with friends than the other. You might have already experienced resentment of your partner's time with friends. Or your partner might feel frustrated by your lack of understanding when he or she wants to be with friends. Discuss together why and when resentment might arise and how you should communicate it and respond to it. How can you reach a compromise or place of mutual respect and understanding?

113. *Do I have any friends you don't like or feel uncomfortable around? If so, why?*

Sometimes one or more of your friends might irritate or annoy your spouse. Maybe his high school buddy is too loud or her best friend tends to gossip too much. Maybe you don't trust or respect one of your partner's friends. Do you feel so uncomfortable around this friend that it's negatively impacting your relationship? Discuss this together and how you both can understand the other's position. How can you make it more comfortable and acceptable for both of you?

114. *How often should we spend time with friends as couples?*

If you have couple friends, it's fun to go out as a foursome or in a group to socialize. However, socializing with other couples can become a method to avoid talking and connecting with each other. You need time with friends, but you also need to have time alone as a couple. One of you might be the "social director" and arrange plans with others every weekend. One of you might enjoy quieter, more spontaneous free time. Discuss how much time each of you thinks is optimal to spend with couple friends.

115. What are your favorite things to do with our couple friends?

When you do go out with friends, you might find yourselves doing the same activities over and over. Or maybe one of you arranges the events, and the other just goes along. Other couples can open the door to fun, new activities, and experiences you might not have considered before. Talk together about what each of you enjoys doing with other couples and the favorite couples you enjoy spending time with.

116. How often do you feel comfortable having friends in our home?

One great way to socialize with friends is by inviting them to your home. Of course, this involves some amount of cleaning and preparation. It also means you might not be able to follow your regular schedule for time together, reading, working on projects, alone time, or your normal bedtime routine. Discuss together how often you'd like to have friends over to socialize. Are there friends you prefer to socialize with at your home rather than outside of it?

117. Which of our friends could you see us traveling with?

Traveling with friends can be fun and create opportunities for shared adventures and memories. However, travel can be stressful, and even the closest couples can find they differ in routines, interests, and stress tolerance. If you think you might enjoy traveling with others, discuss who both of you see as good companions for you. Think about all the possible difficulties related to travel and how this couple might respond to them.

118. How do you feel about me having friends who are the opposite sex?

Perhaps one or both of you had a friend of the opposite sex prior to becoming a couple. Or maybe you've made a friend at work or through a hobby that you have a platonic, enjoyable connection with. Find out from your partner how he or she feels about this friendship now or if you developed a friendship in the future with someone of the opposite sex. What boundaries would you need to set around this kind of friendship? Would it be acceptable at all?

119. Do you feel jealous of any of my friendships, and if so, why?

Sometimes one partner can feel jealous of the closeness shared between the other person and a friend. Perhaps your partner shares feelings or information with a friend that she hasn't shared with you, or maybe he has told his friend too many personal details about your relationship. Maybe you feel as though your spouse enjoys her friendship time more than she enjoys time with you. Ask each other this question and listen without defensiveness to the reason your partner feels this jealousy. How can you address this issue?

120. How can we become better friends to each other?

An intimate love relationship should be grounded in a deep and abiding friendship. Friends have each other's backs and support the other one in good times and bad. Friends enjoy fun times together and have mutual interests and values. Friends are forgiving and compassionate. How do each of you need to be a better friend to your partner? How can you strengthen the bonds of friendship within the context of your romantic relationship?

Follow-up: Are there any behavior adjustments you'd like to request from your partner related to friends and spending time with friends? What specific action steps will you both take to improve your understanding of each other and yourselves related to your friendships and the friendship you have as a couple? Write these down and determine how and when you will initiate these changes or actions.

Section 13: Extended Family

121. How much time should we spend with our extended families (parents, siblings, etc.)?

Sometimes extended family can create tension and frustration with a couple. One of you might want to spend more time with your parents or siblings than the other. One partner might feel unhappy with family members dropping by uninvited or with a practice of spending time with extended family every week. Discuss with each other how you envision the ideal amount of time to spend with extended family (both sets), and any underlying feelings that might create tension around this situation.

122. What holidays or traditions do you feel strongly we spend with your extended family?

Both of you might have holiday traditions with your family of origin that are meaningful and important to you. Or one of you might feel strongly that you build new traditions with your own family that don't always involve your parents or siblings. Discuss with each other what is important to you related to holidays and traditions and why it's so important. How can you each honor the other's wishes and reach a compromise?

123. How should we communicate to the extended family about our new family traditions and create our family boundaries?

Sometimes your extended family has expectations about how you spend your holidays or create family traditions. They might assume you will spend every holiday together or want you to travel to their home exclusively for holidays. It's difficult to communicate your boundaries and differing desires when you know your family might not receive it well. How can you support each other when communicating this to your family? Should one or both of you participate in the conversation?

124. How can we work it out, if we disagree about the amount of time spent with our extended family?

Before you encounter another difficult situation related to time spent with your extended family, discuss a plan in advance for working through future disagreements. Is it acceptable for one of you to spend time with extended family without the other?

Can you reach a middle ground without resentment? Write down a plan so you have a guide when you are in the heat of a decision about a specific situation in the future.

125. How do we handle behavior, expectations, or demands that we don't like from our extended family?

Your mom might indulge your children more than you wish. You dad might insert himself in your financial decisions. Maybe one of your siblings asks you to babysit too often. Inevitably something will arise with an extended family member that causes tension. It's especially difficult to address if the family member is an in-law. If one or both of you is more passive in dealing with conflict, it can cause simmering resentment with your spouse. What are some of the situations you don't want to occur with extended family? Discuss how you would like to resolve these and who will lead the conversation with them.

126. How can we make sure we put our relationship before our extended families?

Conflict and differences related to extended family and in-laws can cause real problems in your relationship. When you have split loyalties, it becomes even more difficult to resolve these problems, as you feel ambivalent about the best course of action. However, if you both agree the health of your relationship comes first, then you can always find a way out of the difficulty. During any given situation, ask yourselves, "What outcome is best for the good of our relationship?" If you can't figure this out together, work with a counselor to help you. Don't allow conflict or resentment to simmer.

127. Is there anything I do that makes you feel I don't put you ahead of my extended family?

This is a good time to discuss any underlying resentments either of you might have about how your partner relates to extended family. Listen openly and compassionately to each other about any negative feelings, even if you feel defensive or hurt. Allow your partner to fully express his or her feelings and acknowledge those feelings without judgment. Sometimes simply listening and acknowledging is all that's needed to heal an issue. But discuss any specific changes or actions your partner might request from you and consider what you are willing to change.

128. How would you like me to handle it, if someone in my family says or does something to offend you, in person or behind your back?

In some families, one or more members might be passively or openly rude or hostile to your spouse or partner. They might complain about your spouse to other family members or make snide remarks in your presence or your partner's presence. If this occurs, ask your spouse how he or she wants to handle the situation. Does she want you to speak up, or does she want to handle it? How can you both prevent the situation from occurring again or getting worse? What is the bottom line for both of you, and what will you do if the situation doesn't improve?

129. Who in our family would best serve as guardians for our children?

It's difficult to think about needing guardians for your children, but you want your children cared for in a loving environment should the worst happen. Optimally, it would be best if your children went to a family member with whom they are close and feel happy and comfortable. But the family member needs to be willing and able to raise your children. Is there anyone in either of your extended families who would best serve as guardians for your children? Discuss together what you both consider to be the ideal guardian situation, and who in your family (or friends, if necessary) would come closest to fitting that scenario.

130. What is your rule as a couple about discussing marital problems with extended family?

If you are close with your parents or siblings, they might be the first people you call when you and your partner are having problems. This can cause divisiveness between your spouse and your family, even after you and your spouse resolve the conflict. Discuss together what you feel is acceptable when it comes to talking about your marriage or your partner's behaviors with your extended family members.

Follow-up: Are there any behavior adjustments you'd like to request from your partner related to extended family and spending time with extended family? What specific action steps will you both take to improve your understanding of each other and yourselves related to your families and how you interact with them? Write these down and determine how and when you will initiate these changes or actions.

Section 14: Spiritual Life and Values

131. What are your top five personal values?

Your core values are the guiding principles of your life. They represent what is most important to you and how you want to spend your time. If either of you haven't defined your core values, review the list of 400 value words on my website to help you determine your top five to ten core values (see Resources). Share your list of top values with each other.

132. What should be our most important values as a couple?

Your individual values may not be exactly the same as your values as a couple. As a team, you might have values that support and honor your relationship and family. Review the list of values together and determine your top five to ten values as a committed couple. Start by selecting all the values that seem important, then hone them to the most important few.

133. How are we prioritizing our values in our life and family?

After you determine your values as individuals and as a couple, examine your lifestyle, behaviors, and choices to see how you are currently living in alignment with those values. Honoring your values as a couple and individually is critical to living authentically and happily. Ask your partner how he or she perceives you, related to honoring your individual core values. Sometimes your loved one can see you more objectively than you can see yourself.

134. What do we need to change to live closer to our values?

The previous exercise will likely highlight where you aren't honoring your core values. What is happening in your lives or relationship that undermines one or more of these values? Discuss what is getting in the way of living in alignment with your values, and what actions you need to take to improve that.

135. How important is your spiritual life, and how do you practice it?

Even if you've discussed this prior to committing as a couple, it's important to revisit your feelings about

your spiritual life. Throughout the years, your beliefs and practices might change. One of you might
have differing spiritual needs or beliefs. Maybe one
of you has felt uncomfortable discussing this. Give
each other the freedom and respect to openly discuss the importance (or lack of importance) of your
spiritual lives.

136. What should we do as a couple to enhance our spiritual lives together?

Where do your spiritual or religious views overlap?
It might be something as simple as spending time
in nature together or reading an inspiring poem out
loud before bed. Maybe you want to pray together
or attend services more often as a couple. Connecting as a couple to something deeply meaningful and larger than yourselves is an important way
to create intimacy and connection, even if you don't
completely agree on spiritual matters.

137. If we don't share the same spiritual or religious views, how is this impacting our relationship?

If you have differences related to your religious or spiritual views, consider how these differences are impacting your love and respect for each other. Some couples can easily hold different views and maintain an intimate, bonded connection. However, if one or both of you feels resentful, worried, or frustrated by the other's views or beliefs, this can create a divide between you. You might discover it's best to agree to disagree, as attempting to sway your partner to embrace your beliefs can backfire. Mutual respect and acceptance is generally the best path for the health of your relationship.

138. How would you react if my religious or spiritual views changed, and we no longer shared the same views?

Your beliefs and views can change, and this can be disconcerting to the spouse who still holds the same beliefs you once held. Religious beliefs can be so important to some people that they will only marry someone of the same faith. If you are in the position that you no longer share the same faith, and it's causing distress for both of you, then counseling is definitely in order. Trying to force someone to believe or disbelieve will never work. People's views about faith and religion are uniquely their own. Counseling can help you find a way to navigate your religious differences and save the relationship.

139. What religious or spiritual beliefs do you have from your primary family that might no longer work for you?

More often than not, our religious views were adopted from our family of origin. If you were raised Jewish, Christian, Hindu, or nothing at all, then you likely had (or still have) these beliefs. However, as we get older, we might change our views and see that the beliefs of our parents are not our beliefs any longer. Maybe you or your spouse feels this way but has never articulated it. Give each other a safe and nonjudgmental space to talk about this and how it feels to diverge from the family's beliefs.

140. What spiritual or religious views do we want to teach our children?

Perhaps this is something you discussed early in your marriage or relationship. If so, are you honoring your own desires related to teaching your children particular religious or spiritual views? Is one of you more responsible for this than the other, and is that acceptable to both of you? If you haven't had this conversation before, then this is a good time to discuss how you want to involve and educate your children in spiritual or religious matters.

Follow-up: Are there any behavior adjustments you'd like to request from your partner related to your spiritual life and values? What specific action steps will you both take to improve your understanding of each other and yourselves related to your values and spirituality? Write these down and determine how and when you will initiate these changes or actions.

Section 15: Health and Fitness

141. What can we do as a couple to create a healthier lifestyle?

You owe it not only to yourself but to your partner to be in good health. Being healthy and energetic makes a huge difference in your state of mind and overall happiness. Are both of you committed to a healthy lifestyle? Do you both want to maintain the proper weight, eat the right foods, exercise, stay current with check-ups, and avoid risky behaviors or overindulging in alcohol or recreational drugs? How can you support each other in these choices?

142. What physical activities could we do together to improve our fitness?

A healthy lifestyle must include some physical activity, whether it's walking, running, biking, going to the gym, or playing a sport. Doing these activities together not only improves your health and well-being, but also strengthens the bonds of your intimacy and connection. Talk about the activities you would enjoying doing together as a couple and how you are going to commit to making this part of your lives.

143. What specifically could we change about our eating habits or diet that would be healthier?

It's easy to say, "Let's eat a healthier diet," but what does that mean specifically? Will you stop buying junk food, soda, or sweets? Will you increase the amounts of fruits and vegetables in your diet? Will you reduce portion sizes or cut back on late-night snacking? Maybe it means you go grocery shopping together and plan your meals in advance. Discuss your individual ideas for a healthy diet and how you can find common ground.

144. How should we handle it, if our health and fitness goals are different?

For some couples, the differences in attitude about health and fitness can be as difficult to navigate as religious differences or differing sexual needs. If one of you holds fitness as a primary value while the other is more casual about it, this can be the source of resentment or conflict. One partner might take up a sport that the other doesn't enjoy. Or if one of you has a more extreme diet preference, like being a raw vegan for example, then the other can feel frustrated by the limited food choices you can enjoy as a couple. You both know that health and fitness are important, so create a goal of meeting in the middle during certain times of the week. Discuss how you feel about your differing goals and what you need from each other to feel comfortable.

145. How do you want me to treat you, when you feel sick or have an illness?

When we're in poor health or have an illness, we need our partner's support and love more than usual. For some, that love and support means being physically present, offering acts of extra kindness and care, and speaking words of comfort. For others, it might mean being left alone and remaining quiet during recuperation. Find out from your spouse what he or she needs and wants from you during times of illness or feeling poorly.

146. Do I have any bad health habits that really bother you? If so, what are they?

It can be uncomfortable to say to your partner, "I think you need to lose some weight," or "You really drink more than I feel comfortable with." Whether your partner's bad health habit directly impacts you or not, you want him or her to have the self-respect to care for themselves and be healthy and happy for you. When asking each other this question, you might hear something that is hurtful or embarrassing. Be gentle and loving as you share your answers and open-minded when you hear them.

147. How can I ask you to work on a bad health habit I observe in you?

This issue might come up again in the future if you observe your partner making a health choice that isn't ideal or that really bothers you. You both need the freedom to discuss this without it turning into an argument or without embarrassing or judging each other. If your partner is frustrated or concerned about one of your habits, how would you like him or her to approach you and voice the concern?

148. How are we serving as healthy role models for our children and extended family and friends?

Every choice you make and habit you practice is a message to those around you about who you are and what you value. What kind of couple do you want to be for those who are paying close attention to your choices and actions? What do you want to teach your children through your behaviors and how do you want your friends and family to perceive you when it relates to health and physical well-being?

149. If you could improve one thing related to your health and fitness, what would it be?

Hopefully you've created goals as a couple around

good health and fitness, but you likely also have personal goals. There are some health habits that are keystone habits—habits that trigger you to perform other healthy behaviors. For example, exercise might trigger you to cut out unhealthy foods from your diet. What might be a keystone habit for you?

150. How can I help and support you to achieve that one thing?

As we work toward our individual goals around health and fitness, we need the support and accountability our partner can provide us. Find out specifically how you can offer this support as your loved one pursues a keystone health or fitness habit. Are you willing to provide the support requested, and if not, what are you willing to do to help him or her reach their goal?

Follow-up: Are there any behavior adjustments you'd like to request from your partner related to your health and fitness? What specific action steps will you both take to improve your health and fitness as a couple and as individuals? Write these down and determine how and when you will initiate these changes or actions.

Section 16: Work

151. How does your work (in a profession or as a parent/homemaker) impact your overall happiness in our life together?

Does the work you do, whether inside or outside the home, add to your happiness and therefore to the happiness of your lives as a couple? Explain to each other specifically how your jobs make your lives better or worse. In what positive or negative ways are you impacted by your job and how does that spill over to your life together?

152. What makes you most happy and unhappy with your job?

Most jobs have positive and negative aspects, but hopefully the good far outweighs the bad. Talk about what you love about your work and what you don't enjoy. Are you passionate about the work you do, or do you feel unfulfilled and bored? Does your work come close to your vision of a fulfilling career? Discuss the specifics of what fills you up and why, in addition to what saps your energy and stresses you. Listen intently to each other as you share this information.

153. How can I best support you in your work?

Work is a huge part of our lives and impacts our state of mind and our quality of life. We have good days and bad days on our jobs, and we all need to share these experiences and our feelings about them with our intimate partner. Find out how you can offer not only a listening ear, but also ongoing support, feedback, and counsel to your spouse related to his or her job. How can you both help each other find more fulfillment in the work you do?

154. If your unhappiness at work is impacting our relationship or family, what would you be willing to do to address the problem?

If you are unhappy at work, it's hard to stay positive and upbeat when you come home. Your unhappiness is bound to affect your state of mind and your ability to interact with your spouse and family in a healthy way. This is manageable for the short term, but over time, your unhappiness, complaints, and negative mood will undermine your relationships. If this is happening now or there might be a possibility it can happen in the future, what are you willing to do to change the situation? Discuss possible alternatives together, such as changing jobs, counseling, or making an entire career change.

155. How can you manage stress from your job, so it doesn't impact our life at home?

If one of you is unhappy on the job now but truly can't do anything about it in the near future, then you'll need a plan for coping with the stress and frustration. Part of managing the stress is working together to brainstorm a future exit strategy or reevaluating your mutual priorities to facilitate change more quickly. On a day-to-day basis, what habits or practices can you employ so your unhappiness doesn't undermine the health of your relationship and family life? These might include exercise, meditation, visualization, simplifying your life, and incorporating more fun activities into your free time.

156. How many hours a day is enough for you to spend at work?

Problems often occur in relationships when one person spends more hours on the job than the other partner is comfortable with. Or one partner might need to travel regularly, impacting the amount of time you spend together as a couple or as a family. This could be a requirement of the job, or it might be by choice, but either way if it's negatively impacting the relationship, you need to address it.

Find out from each other how many hours a day (and a week) is preferred and how you both think you're doing in sticking to that amount.

157. How should we handle it, if I feel you are spending too much time at work and not enough time with me?

One of you might feel unhappy or frustrated with the amount of time the other spends at work. You might even feel he or she is choosing work over your relationship. When these feelings arise, you need to address them and listen compassionately to each other. Talk about how to work through this problem should it arise for one or both of you. How can both of you get your needs met and feel you are living up to your work obligations and responsibilities?

158. Where do you see yourself in your career in the next five years? The next ten?

Your careers impact the vision you have for your lives as a couple. If you have a vision to start a family, buy a house, travel, or build your own business, what you plan now related to your career will help both of you attain your vision. Where do you and your partner envision yourselves with your careers during the next five to ten years? How do you plan to make it happen? Both you and your spouse should be involved in planning your career goals and the actions you take toward achieving them.

159. How much job security do you think you have?

Do you feel strongly your job will be there for you for years to come, or is it possible you could lose your job or your employer or business could fail in the next year or two? If you don't feel completely secure in your job, discuss this with your spouse, and brainstorm how you both could prepare for the worst-case scenario if it occurs. What will you live on? Will your partner's salary cover your expenses for a while? Do you need to save money for an emergency fund if you should need it?

160. What is your plan should you decide to leave your job?

If one of you decides to voluntarily leave his or her job to pursue something else, what plans are place? Having a plan in place affords the security and freedom to initiate change when you want to change jobs, stay at home to care for kids, start a business, or retire. Do you see this possibility in your short-term future (the next five years)? If so, what needs to be done in order to make a smooth transition and maintain (or alter) your lifestyle to accommodate any salary changes?

Follow-up: Are there any behavior adjustments you'd like to request from your partner related to your careers? What specific action steps will you both take to support each other's career goals and manage your own stress related to your work? Write these down and determine how and when you will initiate these changes or actions.

Section 17: Children and Parenting

161. What are our guiding principles as parents?

Have you given thought as a couple about how you want to raise your children and parent them on a day-to-day basis? Do you have a philosophy you both embrace that serves as a foundation for making parenting decisions? Discuss together what your primary parenting values are and how you want to apply them in the daily work of raising your kids—from how you deal with behavior problems to the way you instill values in them.

162. What do you see as my best parenting skills?

If you are parents, find out from your spouse what he or she believes are your strongest skills in parenting. Give specific instances of how your partner applied these skills with your children. Talk about how and why both of you have something unique to offer as parents and how your children will benefit from what you both bring to the table. Acknowledge and compliment each other for contributing these positive qualities, boundaries, and emotions to your children's lives.

163. Where do you struggle most in parenting our children?

Children go through different life stages, and some of them are more difficult for parents than others. They can test our patience and best intentions. We can stray from our vision of who we want to be with our kids and how we want to raise them. Learn from each other what each of you struggles with in raising your kids right now. Do you both struggle with the same difficulties, or can one of you step in where the other feels weak? How can you support each other in these struggles?

164. What parenting skills from your parents do you want to emulate with our children?

Think about the way your parents raised you and what they got right. It's often not until we have children ourselves that we appreciate all that our parents did for us and why they made the decisions they did. How were your parents good role models for you as you strive to be a good parent? Talk together about what positive parenting skills you want to adopt from your parents and use together with your children.

165. What do you want to do differently from your parents?

No parent gets it right all the time, and often siblings in the same family require different parenting skills. You might have felt misunderstood, unfairly punished, ignored, or harshly treated by your parents. Maybe you didn't like the rules in your household or felt one parent was too strict. If your parents had a style that you dislike, you might unconsciously find yourself emulating it. Ask each other this question so you can carefully consider what you don't want to replay with your own children.

166. How do we handle disagreements related to parenting our children effectively?

There will be times when you disagree about an issue with your children. It's important both for your relationship and for your child's sense of security that you present a united front and not argue about a parenting issue in front of your child. That said, decide now how you will handle these disagreements, where you'll have the conversation, and what you'll do if you can't work out a mutually agreeable solution.

167. How can we manage the stresses of parenting so we don't take it out on each other?

Children afford a lot of joy and satisfaction, but having children changes your romantic relationship. You no longer have the time and freedoms you had when it was just the two of you. You have many more life demands and situations that cause conflict, anxiety, and stress. As the heads of your family, the two of you need to maintain a close, peaceful relationship so you can support each other and create an emotionally healthy environment for your kids. What are some specific actions you can take when the demands of parenting become too much?

168. How can I best support you as a co-parent in this family, particularly when you feel stressed?

Maybe you come home from work exhausted, and the kids are fighting while you're trying to fix dinner. Or perhaps your daughter asks for help with her homework, but you're overwhelmed trying to pay the bills. There are times when we know we need to be there for our kids, but we just don't have the energy to step up. Those are the times when your partner or spouse can step in and offer support or verbally reinforce your decision or rules. Discuss circumstances when this has happened in the past or might happen in the future. What specific kinds of parenting support do each of you need from the other during stressful times?

169. What are some specific ways we can put our relationship first so our household isn't "child centered"?

Children feel most secure when it's clear that their parents are a couple before they are parents. They need to know who sets the rules and who is in charge. Children need adults to step up and show them that they don't rule the family through their wants or behaviors. Your relationship as a couple sets the stage for the happiness of the entire family. How are you putting your relationship first? What boundaries are you setting with your children to re-inforce that your connection as a couple is primary? Discuss some specific things you want to do to establish your family as "parent-centered."

170. What do we agree we will never say or do in front of our children?

In addition to working out parenting conflict privately, what else do you both wish to handle or do without your children present? It's certainly OK to work out conflict in front of them in a calm way, but you likely don't want them to witness you yelling at each other or behaving badly. Talk together about what you don't want to say or do around your kids and what you'll do in the heat of the moment if they observe you.

Follow-up: Are there any behavior adjustments you'd like to request from your partner related to your children? What specific action steps will you both take to support each other as parents and maintain the integrity of your relationship as a couple? Write these down and determine how and when you will initiate these changes or actions.

Section 18: Money

171. What are your long-term financial goals for us?

Do each of you have specific financial goals for the future? What do you want your net worth to be? Have you thought about saving for a major purchase or for your children's education? Have you put together a retirement plan? Is there debt that needs to be paid off? You might have differing financial goals, or one of you might have considered these goals and the other isn't focused on it. As a couple, you need to be on the same page about your financial goals and how you are going to reach them.

172. What should we do to stay on top of our financial goals?

Once you discuss your financial goals and come to an agreement on what your joint goals should be, think about the specific actions and plans you want to implement to make those goals happen. How and when will you implement them? Who will be in charge of taking the actions? Even if one of you is more active with financial planning than the other, it's important that all plans and decisions are made together. Neither of you wants to feel an "imbalance of power" when it comes to your finances.

173. What are your values and beliefs about money?

Our personalities, families of origin, and life experiences determine our attitudes about money. Some people view it as a scarce resource and hold tightly to what they have. Others see money as always available and abundant and have few fears about spending. Some see making money as an interesting pursuit while others view it simply as a means to an end. As a couple you have an obligation to balance your values and beliefs to find common ground between you. Talk about your attitude related to money with your partner and how you developed the values and beliefs you have.

174. What causes you the most worry or frustration about money now?

Wherever you are in your life right now, you likely have some concerns about money. Maybe you want to make more. Maybe you're concerned about your debt. It could be that you worry about the stock market and how your money is performing. Allow your partner to express his or her worries and just listen without passing judgment or reinforcing those concerns. Ask your partner if he or she wants to discuss possible ways to address the worries.

175. How are our spending and saving habits complementary?

Talk together about the way you both handle money and how your habits are similar. In what areas of spending and saving do you both agree? For now, just talk about the common ground and how you are alike in this regard. Even if you have differences in how you handle money, it's important to focus on the similarities and see that you share common values and behaviors.

176. How are our spending and saving habits different?

You will likely have areas of difference in your spending and saving habits. These differences might have caused conflict or resentment in the past. Without pointing fingers or getting defensive, simply articulate how you are different. Then ask your spouse more about the emotions behind his or her habits. Money habits often have emotional drivers. For example, you might ask, "How does it make you feel to put $500 in savings every month?" or "What is the deeper reason you want to buy a new car rather than a used one?" Ask these questions with the real intention of understanding the feelings behind the behaviors.

177. How should we handle it if we have a disagreement about money?

Having a better understanding of your spouse's values and emotions about money can help you manage disagreements about it. If you have defined your values as a couple and you agree on your financial goals for the future, you should be able to return to those for guidance in addressing disagreements. This requires you are both equally committed to your mutual values and goals. However, there will be exceptions and times each of you might want to stray from your goals for a new priority or opportunity. Talk about how you can address these future issues without it becoming a heated discussion involving blame or shame. Determine your hot buttons about money conflict and how you can avoid these hot buttons and have a productive conversation.

178. What kind of debt do you feel is acceptable for us?

Some people don't want any debit except their mortgage. Others are fine using credit cards, financing their car, or taking out a student loan. What are your individual attitudes about debt and how much you should carry as a couple? If you disagree about this, how can you determine an acceptable amount of debt? Once you mutually determine this, are you both committed to sticking to the agreement?

179. How much money should we save each month?

Saving money is essential for reaching your financial goals and dealing with any unexpected emergencies or life priorities. If you are living beyond your means or have debt, you need to address these. But it's still important to get into the habit of putting money aside, even if it's a small amount. Based on your financial goals and your current level of debt, you should have some idea of how much you should save. This might require you to cut back on expenses or alter your lifestyle. Are you both willing to do this? Discuss together how much you believe is realistic to set aside each month.

180. Do you feel on top of our finances and know where our money is going? If not, how can I help you be more aware of this?

Sometimes one partner is more involved and informed related to finances than the other. It's easy to fall into a pattern of allowing this partner to handle everything without being involved in decisions or understanding where your money goes each month. However, you both need to feel invested in financial decisions and have a basic understanding of your expenses, investments, and debts. If this is the situation in your relationship, make it a point to bring your partner up to speed, even if he or she hasn't asked you to do this.

Follow-up: Are there any financial concerns you'd like to better understand from your partner's viewpoint? What specific action steps will you both take to support each other in your financial goals as a couple? Write these down and determine how and when you will initiate these changes or actions.

Section 19: Life Crises

181. How have you reacted in the past to serious life problems , such as a death or job loss?

It's inevitable that some life crises will occur during your lives together as a couple. Maybe you've already experienced a tragic or disruptive life event that has tested you as individuals and as a couple. Talk with each other about how you each tend to react, feel, and behave during a crisis. Your reactions might be different depending on the type of event (a job loss compared to the death of a loved one, for example). Consider the possible serious life events you might face together, discuss these, and try to understand how your partner will respond if these should occur.

182. How can I support you during a time of crisis?

Once you've discussed past and possible future serious life crises, ask your partner what he or she might need from you in way of support and compassion. For example, if your partner loses a parent or gets fired from a job, what specific actions or attitudes would he or she need from you? If a life event is equally devastating to both of you (you lose a beloved pet or your mutual business fails, for example), how can you be there for each other and

get the emotional support you need as individuals?
Before you are blindsided by a crisis, talk about
your support plan.

183. How could we prepare for a job loss or financial crisis?

In previous questions, you've addressed the practical actions of planning for financial emergencies.
But how can you plan for the emotional aspects if
one of loses a job or suffers a serious financial
loss? These situations usually create issues about
confidence, self-esteem, fear, self-doubt, and lack
of motivation. Should this kind of crisis occur, what
are your likely responses, both as the one most directly affected and as the supportive partner? What
will you need to do create a softer landing and to
reduce stress during these times? What outside
support from friends, family, or professionals might
you need?

184. If I had a life-threatening illness, how would you react and cope?

No one wants to consider the possibility of a loved
one having a serious illness or disability. But these
situations occur, and it's valuable to understand
how your partner might react in this situation and
what coping mechanisms he or she might employ.
How much care-giving is your partner willing and

able to do? How does illness in the house make him or her feel? Who would he or she call on for emotional and/or physical support? An important part of this discussion is sharing what both of you want in the way of a living will and any other specific end-of-life wishes.

185. What kind of crisis could potentially harm our relationship, and how would we handle it?

When a crisis occurs, the fear and pain often makes us lash out at the one we are closest to. We are looking for someone to blame, and this person is the easiest target. Some serious crises are known to pull couples apart (like the death of a child, for example), but if you recognize this as a possibility and proactively deal with the feelings of anger and pain, you can save your relationship, and in some cases make your relationship stronger. Do you envision any crisis situations in which your relationship might be in jeopardy? Talk about these and how you would address the problem.

186. What do we need to do to plan and prepare should one or both of us die unexpectedly?

If your partner were to die today, do you know how to access all of his or her important information and documents? Are you up-to-speed on where all of your financial information is? Do you have a will prepared and have you established guardians for your children? Should this tragedy occur, the last thing you or someone in your family will want to do is scramble around for directives, documents, and passwords. As uncomfortable as it is, you need to discuss these preparations and when you plan to take care of them.

187. How do you grieve the loss of something or someone you cherish?

We all grieve differently. Some of us openly express our pain and allow tears to flow freely, while others go within and suffer in silence. Loss doesn't always mean the loss of someone you care about. We can grieve the loss of our youth, moving from one home to another, or our kids leaving home. Understanding how your partner grieves and what his or her grief looks like can help you be more compassionate, supportive, and empathetic.

188. What life crisis do you fear the most? Why?

Most of us have that one big fear that puts a knot in our stomach or creates low-level anxiety. Maybe it's getting cancer, losing a child, or your business failing. Find out what your partner fears the most and why he or she has so much fear about this particular crisis. By talking about our fears in a safe and loving environment, it can actually lessen the anxiety and make us feel more in control.

189. What else can we do to prepare or protect ourselves from unexpected crises?

Discuss if there are any practical or emotional actions you need to take to prepare or protect yourself from a life crisis or tragedy. For example, maybe you're living in an unsafe area, and you need to consider moving. Maybe one of you has a job that is risky physically or financially, and you should consider changing jobs. Your car might have bald tires, and you need a new set. In what ways might you be putting yourselves at risk for tragedy that you can address by taking action now?

190. How can we adopt a "growth mindset" when a big life crisis occurs?

A growth mindset means you believe you have the ability to not only survive the crisis, but also to learn and grow from it. Growth-minded people recognize they have the inner resources to move past a crisis after an appropriate period of grief and pain. It involves practicing optimism and hope, allowing yourself to fully feel and express your emotions, and finding a great meaning in your struggle. Do you practice a growth mindset during the small difficulties of your life? How can you work together as a couple to practice optimism and reinforce your ability to handle whatever life throws at you?

Follow-up: Are there any life crises you'd like to better understand from your partner's viewpoint? What specific action steps will you both take to support each other in these life concerns as a couple? Write these down and determine how and when you will initiate these changes or actions.

Section 20: Goals and Dreams

191. What kind of legacy do we want to leave our children and the world?

Part of living a fulfilled and happy life is feeling that you are making a meaningful contribution to the world in some way. It could be through your job, raising your children well, through some outside interest or hobby you find meaningful or service-oriented, or simply in the way you live your life. Ask you partner what mark he or she wants to leave on the world after he or she dies. How do you want your children and family to remember you?

192. If you didn't have the job you have now, what would be your dream career?

You might enjoy your job, or it might be far from ideal, but if you had the option to change careers today, what would you do? What did you dream of being when you were a child? If you had all of the talent, ability, skills, and education necessary for a particular career, what would it be? Allow each other to fantasize and brainstorm about your dreams for the perfect career.

193. *What are ten things on your bucket list?*

We all have hopes and dreams for things we want to accomplish, places we want to visit, and things we want to see. Both of you take a minute and write down ten items for your bucket list. Then take turns sharing what's on your list. Where is there cross-over between your items? Are there bucket list items you want to share as a couple? Which items are you ready to prioritize and plan out for the near future (in the next year or two)?

194. *If we won the lottery, what would you want to do with the money?*

This is a fun question to stimulate imagination and express your wildest dreams. Come up with a specific amount of money you might win, and talk together about how you'd want to use the money. Enjoy thinking about the freedom and opportunity you'd have with all the money you'd win. Aside from spending on your own desires, how could you use the money to help others, create something useful, or leave a legacy?

195. Who would you like to spend more time with, and what relationships would you like to develop?

Do you have relationships with friends, business associates, and family that you'd like to strengthen? Are there new friendships you'd like to develop or old friends you'd like to reconnect with? Think about what you are missing in your social life and personal relationships and what you'd like to do to find more joy and depth in your various relation-ships. Ask how you can help your partner reach his or her goals and wishes concerning these relation-ships.

196. If we didn't live in this city, where would you like to live?

There are so many beautiful, interesting, exciting places to live in the world. You might live in your city because it was where you grew up, you found a job there, or maybe you moved to be with your partner. If the world was your oyster, where would you settle down? Think about your ideal lifestyle and the kinds of people and activities you enjoy. What cities best match those? Do you envision ever moving to another city?

197. *If you didn't have to work, how would you spend your time?*

If going to work were optional, but you still received your paycheck, how would you spend your time? What activities would bring you fulfillment and joy? How would your lives be different? Talk together about perfect lifestyle for you as a couple if you could reclaim the hours a day you work.

198. *What do you feel most proud of?*

You have both had many accomplishments and achievements throughout your lives. Which of these, whether in your youth or adulthood, has made you the most proud? Why did it make you feel proud? Listen to each other tell the story of this special moment and acknowledge the accomplishment and feelings your partner shares.

199. *What do you personally want to achieve during the next five to ten years?*

Both of you might have personal goals you've been nurturing. Maybe you want to run a marathon, write a book, or learn to speak a language. Share your personal goals with your partner and find out how you can support each other in reaching those goals. Is there anything getting in the way of attainting your goals, and, if so, what can you both do to address these roadblocks?

200. What do you see us doing during our retirement years?

For some people, retirement means moving to the mountains or the beach and enjoying uninterrupted free time. For others it might mean traveling the world or starting a nonprofit. Talk about how you both envision your retirement years. Where would you live? How would you spend your time? If you differ in your vision, how can you create a retirement scenario that works for both of you?

201. How can we continue to improve our relationship and become closer, kinder, and more intimate?

By working through these questions together, you have initiated a new level of intimacy, compassion, and understanding between you. A love relationship is a work in progress, and, like a garden, it needs constant attention and care. What are your ongoing goals for the health of your relationship? Where do you see areas that need improvement and what specific actions can you work on daily? As individuals, what do each of you need to work on related to anger, emotional reactivity, compassion, kindness, communication, honesty, confidence, trustworthiness, stress, health, reliability, or commitment?

Follow-up: Are there any goals and dreams you'd like to better understand from your partner's viewpoint? What specific action steps will you both take to support each other in your goals as a couple? Write these down and determine how and when you will initiate these changes or actions.

Conclusion:

The Power of Vulnerability

The purpose of these questions has been to strengthen your connection as a couple, to help you better understand each other, and to invite you to take action so you can improve your relationship and deepen your love for each other.

Some of the questions might have touched hot buttons, fears, and areas of pain and shame for both of you. Perhaps it was difficult to navigate these questions and your answers without some defensiveness or anger arising. This tells you where you need some work in the relationship. Remember, behind all those negative reactions is a deeper emotion or need that you might have buried or haven't fully explored. It is through opening up and sharing these deeper emotions with your loved one that you can fully heal. An intimate, loving relationship requires vulnerability.

During a particularly stressful time in my life, my older sister said to me, "Just fall back and let the universe catch you." When she said that, a feeling of peace washed over me. How lovely it would be to simply let go and feel completely safe, knowing that everything would be OK. That I was OK. The thought gave me a few moments of respite from my worries. I was free from the pain and pretense of trying to control everything.

Imagine if you heard those words from the person you love—"Just fall back and let me catch you. Just fall back and tell me everything. Just fall back and be yourself, flaws and all. I will still love you. I will be there for you." Imagine the peace of not holding it all in, of being completely authentic and open, sharing your most intimate dreams and fears, perfectly secure in the knowledge you won't be ridiculed or rejected. Instead you'll be embraced. Imagine being completely vulnerable and exposed, and rather than it pushing your beloved away, it brings you closer together.

Unfortunately, most of us have been trained from an early age not to be vulnerable. We've learned the painful lesson of opening our hearts, telling our truths, and showing our frailties, only to have our hearts broken and our weaknesses disparaged. We've learned to hold back, to pretend to be someone else, to protect our hearts. We've learned that the best defense against pain is a good offense. So we build brick walls. We hold ourselves at arm's length. We offer the smiling, jolly façade, lest others think we aren't pulled together and perfect.

Of course, it's exhausting and stressful maintaining this pretense. It takes a lot of energy to be something you're not. It does protect you from emotional pain in the short term, but in the long run it wreaks havoc on your intimate relationship. Without being vulnerable, intimacy will wither and die, like a flower that never develops deep roots.

Vulnerability is an essential ingredient in your love relationship. Here's why:

Vulnerability reveals reality.

When you are able to show yourself fully to another person, you experience the joy of being fully yourself. And he or she benefits from knowing all of you, not just the glossed-over, flaw-free parts of you. You both enjoy the depths and intricacies of all aspects of each other—the good, bad, and the ugly. There is beauty and security in being known so completely.

Vulnerability fosters trust.

As you reveal yourself to another person, and he or she treats you with respect, love, and dignity, your trust in that person expands. As you reveal more and more of yourself, you also invite the other person to be vulnerable. You give him or her the courage to show the hidden or shameful parts of themselves. Both people experience the security and peace of having the other's back and knowing they are still loved and respected.

Vulnerability invites growth.

Vulnerability allows you to honestly reflect on your true self within the safe harbor of a trusting relationship. You can assess changes you need to make and the person you want to become without taking a blow to your self-esteem. Self-honesty is critical to living authentically, which in turn opens doors to untapped potential.

Vulnerability builds confidence.

As you practice expressing your feelings, revealing your flaws, and admitting your fears, you see that the art of vulnerability actually strengthens you. You realize you can expose yourself without dying or becoming less of a person. You are bolstered by your ability to stand firm in your own truth.

Vulnerability heals wounds.

All healing begins with acknowledgment, acceptance, and awareness. When you are real about your pain or fear, rather than trying to run from it or hide it, you purge yourself of the blocked feelings and stress of trying to pretend or ignore. By putting things out in the open, you allow the light of truth to ignite the healing process.

Vulnerability creates bonds.

All of us have areas of ourselves we fear revealing or sharing with others. We all have pain, shameful feelings, and self-doubt. When you're able to open up about these with another person, you connect with his or her humanness. You allow that individual to see that you are just like them, that you share common feelings and concerns. This bonds you closer to each other.

Vulnerability deepens love.

Vulnerability means you are able to express your deepest feelings for another person and share love on a more profound level. You can be completely open emotionally, mentally, and physically and embrace that same openness from your loved one.

Vulnerability makes us more attractive.

Nothing is more attractive than authenticity. By being fully yourself, and confidently accepting your good and bad qualities, you become more interesting and appealing. Your ability to express yourself openly, share with others, and acknowledge your flaws makes others feel safe and confident around you.

Vulnerability teaches us comfort with uncertainty.

When we are vulnerable, we don't know how others will respond to us. We take a huge risk by putting ourselves out there. This uncertainty causes discomfort and tension. But by practicing vulnerability, we grow accustomed to uncertainty and can tolerate the unpleasant feelings it causes. We can use this new toughness to cope with other areas of risk in our lives that can stretch us and expand opportunities.

As relationship experts Linda and Charlie Bloom remind,

> "The real catastrophe is to come to the end of your life only to realize that by playing it safe and trying to avoid risk, you took the biggest risk of all, and lost the most valuable thing that you could lose: a life that was rich with meaning, feeling, and joy, one that not only filled your

own cup to the brim, but spilled over to fill the cups of others who were moved and inspired by you."

I hope you and your beloved continue to practice vulnerability with each other, and that you offer each other a safe and loving space in which to be yourselves fully without guilt, shame, or judgment. If you meet a roadblock with any of these questions that causes a rift between you, or you can't find a mutually agreeable solution or compromise to a situation, please make it a priority to meet with a licensed relationship counselor to help you. Don't allow discord, misunderstandings, or resentment to fester and undermine the closeness and joy of your relationship.

The love and intimacy you share with each other is the greatest gift you can ever experience. It is the heart of a well-lived, happy life. Treat your relationship with the utmost care, and protect it from the tempests of hurt feelings, misunderstandings, and unkind words. Keep asking questions of each other, and listen with compassion and understanding. Deal with issues quickly and thoroughly. Look for ways to put the relationship first every single day, so you and your partner can enjoy deep and abiding joy, fulfillment, and passion for the rest of your lives.

50 Bonus Questions for Fun

Now that you've completed the more serious work of answering these relationship questions, here are 50 additional questions you can ask to even learn more about your partner and to have some fun together. This is a good time to enjoy an adult beverage (if you drink), put on some music, and share some laughs and memories.

1. How would you describe yourself?

2. What was the happiest moment of your life?

3. What was your most embarrassing moment?

4. What is your first childhood memory?

5. Who has been the most influential person in your life and why?

6. What is something you did as a teenager that your parents never learned about?

7. What's your favorite time of year and why?

8. If you were asked to give yourself a new name, what would it be?

9. If you were asked to give me a new name, what would it be?

10. If we hadn't met each other, where would you be right now?

11. What was on your mind the last time we were having sex?

12. What is your favorite sexual memory of us?

13. What movie reminds you of us?

14. Which of your parents are you most like and in what ways?

15. What is your favorite thing I ever did for a special occasion for you?

16. What's your favorite physical feature on you?

17. Who was your favorite teacher when you were a child?

18. Which significant other before me had the biggest impact on you?

19. What's the angriest you ever felt?

20. Which of your personality traits do you wish you

could change?

21. Which of your parents did you go to when you wanted to talk and why?

22. Which of your friends would you choose if you had to be on a desert island with just one?

23. When you were a kid, did you feel that you fit in? Why or why not?

24. If you could go back in time, what age would you be again?

25. If you could see into the future, what would you want to know?

26. What is the best thing about our relationship?

27. Are you an optimist, a pessimist, or a realist?

28. What things about me make you know I'm the one for you?

29. If our house was on fire and you had a chance to grab only five things before leaving, what would they be?

30. If you could be born again as someone else, who would you be and why?

31. What is your favorite song of all time and why?

32. What is the worst decision you ever made?

33. If you could hand-pick the leader of our country, who would it be and why?

34. What kind of animal do you see yourself as?

35. What kind of animal do you see me as?

36. If you could boil down your life philosophy into one sentence, what would it be?

37. If you could remain one age forever, how old would you be?

38. Would you be willing to live a year in another country where we don't speak the language? Why or why not?

39. If you had one magical superpower, what would it be?

40. How do you think other people perceive you?

41. Aside from me, who really knows you the best?

42. What is the wackiest thing you've ever done?

43. Have you ever had a supernatural or unexplainable experience? If so, what was it?

44. What do you believe happens immediately after we die?

45. In what situations do you feel the most confident and sure of yourself?

46. In what situations do you feel the least confident?

47. What is the best thing you learned from your mom and dad?

48. What one major life regret do you have?

49. On an average day, what do you think about most?

50. What makes you feel most fulfilled in our relationship?

Resources
Your Free Gift

See https://liveboldandbloom.com/free-relation-ship-course

Introduction

Empathic Listening Skills.
See https://liveboldandbloom.com/06/self-improvement/empathic-listening

Section 3

Empathic Listening Article.
See https://liveboldandbloom.com/06/self-improvement/empathic-listening

Section 4

List of Needs.
See https://liveboldandbloom.com/list-of-needs

Section 5

Personal Boundaries.
See https://liveboldandbloom.com/08/life-coaching/want-to-boost-your-self-esteem-10-ways-to-establish-personal-boundaries

Section 7

Summer Activities.
See https://liveboldandbloom.com/03/lifestyle/fun-things-to-do-on-the-weekend

Winter Activities.
See https://liveboldandbloom.com/01/lifestyle/shake-up-your-weekend-25-ways-to-beat-winter-doldrums-and-have-unmitigated-fun

Section 8

Creating Sustainable Habits.
See https://liveboldandbloom.com/09/habits/how-to-create-habits-that-stick

Change Your Mental Attitude.
See http://liveboldandbloom.com/11/mindfulness/positive-mental-attitude

Section 14

List of Value Words.
See https://liveboldandbloom.com/05/values/list-of-values

Sources for Citations

Introduction

Pew Research Center. See http://www.pewsocial-trends.org/2013/02/13/love-and-marriage/

Cornell University Study. See http://www.news.cornell.edu/stories/2005/12/people-committed-relationships-are-happier

Harriet Pappenheim. See http://liveboldandbloom.com/11/relationships/how-to-fix-a-relationship

Section 1

Gary Chapman. See http://www.focusonthefamily.com/marriage/communication-and-conflict/learn-to-speak-your-spouses-love-language/understanding-the-five-love-languages

Section 2

Oxford Dictionary. See http://www.oxforddictionaries.com/us/definition/american_english/respect

Section 6

Every Day Families. See http://www.everydayfami-ly.com/how-often-do-normal-couples-have-sex/?pg=2&internallink=how-often-do-normal-couples-have-sex#post-12063

Conclusion

Linda and Charlie Bloom. See http://www.huffing-tonpost.com/linda-bloom-lcsw-and-charlie-bloom-msw/honesty_b_3696127.html

Want to Learn More?

If you'd like to learn more about self-coaching, powerful questions, relationships, and other personal growth topics, please visit my blog <u>LiveBoldandBloom.com</u> for more articles.

Did You Like
201 Relationship Questions?

Thank you so much for purchasing *201 Relationship Questions: The Couple's Guide to Building
Trust and Emotional Intimacy.* I'm honored by the
trust you've placed in me and my work by choosing
this book to improve your life. I truly hope you've
enjoyed it and found it useful.

I'd like to ask you for a small favor. Would you
please take just a minute to leave a review for this
book on Amazon? This feedback will help me continue to write the kind of books that will best serve
you. If you really loved the book, please let me
know!

Other Books You Might Enjoy from Barrie Davenport

Declutter Your Mind: How to Stop Worrying, Relieve Anxiety, and Eliminate Negative Thinking

Self-Care for Introverts: 17 Soothing Rituals for Peace in a Hectic World

10-Minute Mindfulness: 71 Habits for Living in the Present Moment

Finely-Tuned: How to Thrive as a Highly Sensitive Person or Empath

Peace of Mindfulness: Everyday Rituals to Conquer Anxiety and Claim Unlimited Inner Peace

10-Minute Declutter: The Stress-Free Habit for Simplifying Your Home

Self-Discovery Questions: 155 Breakthrough Questions to Accelerate Massive Action

Building Confidence: Get Motivated, Overcome Social Fear, Be Assertive, and Empower Your Life for Success

201 Relationship Questions

Confidence Hacks: 99 Small Actions to Massively Boost Your Confidence

Sticky Habits: 6 Simple Steps to Create Good Habits that Stick

The 52-Week Life Passion Project

Made in the USA
Columbia, SC
06 July 2019